DATE DUE

The Corridors of Time ·VI·

THE WAY OF THE SEA

By HAROLD PEAKE and
HERBERT JOHN FLEURE

NEW HAVEN · YALE UNIVERSITY PRESS
LONDON · HUMPHREY MILFORD
OXFORD UNIVERSITY PRESS
1929

OXFORD UNIVERSITY PRESS
AMEN HOUSE, E.C. 4
LONDON EDINBURGH GLASGOW
LEIPZIG NEW YORK TORONTO
MELBOURNE CAPETOWN BOMBAY
CALCUTTA MADRAS SHANGHAI
HUMPHREY MILFORD
PUBLISHER TO THE
UNIVERSITY

PRINTED IN GREAT BRITAIN AT THE UNIVERSITY PRESS, OXFORD
BY JOHN JOHNSON, PRINTER TO THE UNIVERSITY

PREFACE

THE disturbances that hindered the development of civilization about the middle of the third millennium B.C. make one of the clearest dividing-lines in the story of ancient times. When the situation again began to clear, it is evident that there was a great increase in the mobility of peoples, that the folk in the Mediterranean basin had awakened to a much more intense life, and that intercourse by sea and land, marked by numerous exchanges of culture, had become a dominant feature.

This volume is concerned mainly with the evidences of this intercourse, and it endeavours to set forth a balanced but provisional view of the basis of civilization in Western Europe, as well as some account of the contemporary life of the peoples of the Near East. It would be possible to argue that the period under consideration in this volume formed the transition from truly ancient times to the dawn of the modern epoch, in which Europe, in spite of many vicissitudes, has been growing in importance, and in which improved means of transport, the horse, the camel, and the ship, have been spreading far and wide the blessings of civilization and the curse of war, while empires, founded upon military power, were growing in importance.

Many thanks are due to the authors, editors, and publishers of the following works and journals for permission to reproduce figures: *The Dawn of European Civilization*, by V. Gordon Childe (Kegan Paul, Trench, Trubner & Co., Ltd.), for figs. 2 *c* and 44 *b*; *Mesopotamia*, by L. Delaporte (Kegan Paul, Trench, Trubner & Co., Ltd.), for fig. 58; *Ilios*, by H. Schliemann (John Murray), for figs. 29 and 33 *f*; *Rude Stone Monuments in all Countries*, by J. Fergusson (John Murray), for fig. 42; *A Guide to the Antiquities of the Stone Age*, 1911 (British Museum), for fig. 52 *b*; *A Catalogue of the Greek and Etruscan Vases in the British Museum*, vol. i, part i, by E. J. Forsdyke (British Museum), for figs. 27 and 31 *b*; *Zeitschrift für Ethnologie*, 1896 (A. Asher & Co., Berlin), for fig. 12 *b*; *Prehistoric Thessaly*, by A. J. B. Wace and M. S. Thompson (Cambridge University Press), for fig. 30; *Scythians and Greeks*, by E. H. Minns (Cambridge University Press), for fig. 11; *A Textbook of European Archaeology*, vol. i, by R. A. S. Macalister (Cambridge University Press), for fig. 44 *a*; *Reallexikon der Vorgeschichte*, vols. i, iv, vii, viii, x, and xi (Walter de Gruyter & Co., Berlin), for figs. 4, 5, 8 *a*, 13, 23, 34 *b–c*, 37, 39 *b–c*, 41 *a–b*, and 47 *c*; *Manuel d'archéologie préhistorique celtique et gallo-romaine*, vol. i, by J. Déchelette (Librairie Alphonse Picard et Fils, Paris), for fig. 40 *a*; *Musée préhistorique*, by G. de Mortillet (E. Arrault et Cie, Tours), for fig. 41 *c–d*; *Corpus of Prehistoric Pottery*, by Professor Sir Flinders Petrie (Bernard

Quaritch, Ltd.), for fig. 6; *Bulletin de la Société d'anthropologie de Bruxelles*, vol. xxxix (Société d'Anthropologie de Bruxelles), for fig. 9; *Archaeologia*, vols. xlii, lxii, lxviii, and lxx (Society of Antiquaries of London), for figs. 14 *a*, *b*, *c*, and *f*, 51 *b*, and 52 *a*; *The Antiquaries Journal*, vol. i (Society of Antiquaries of London), for fig. 52 *d*; *Papers of the British School at Rome*, vol. vi (British School at Rome), for fig. 17; *The Axe Age*, by T. D. Kendrick (Methuen & Co., Ltd.), for figs. 40 *b–c*; *La Cultura del Vaso Campaniforme*, 1928, by A. del Castillo Yurrita (University of Barcelona), for figs. 20, 21*a*, *b* and *d*, 22 *c*, 25, 35, 36, and 38; *The Ancient Implements, Weapons, and Ornaments of Great Britain*, by Sir John Evans (Longmans, Green & Co., Ltd.), for fig. 39 *a*; *Report on the Excavation of the 'A' Cemetery at Kish, Mesopotamia*, part i, by Ernest MacKay (Field Museum of Natural History, Chicago), for fig. 47 *a*; *Man*, vol. xxvii, no. 12 (Royal Anthropological Institute and C. E. Vulliamy), for fig. 54 *c*; *Asia, Europe, and the Aegean, and their Earliest Interrelations* (Studies in Early Pottery of the Near East, ii), by H. Frankfort (Royal Anthropological Institute), for fig. 64; *Early History of Assyria*, by S. Smith (Chatto & Windus), for fig. 61; *A History of Sumer and Akkad*, by L. W. King (Chatto & Windus), for fig. 62; *The Transactions of the Royal Irish Academy*, vol. xxx (Royal Irish Academy), for fig. 55; *A History of Egypt*, by J. H. Breasted (Scribner's Sons, New York), for fig. 71; *Vor Oldtids Mindesmærker*, 1925, by Hans Kjær (Gyldendalske Boghandel Nordisk Forlag, Copenhagen), for fig. 45; *The Vaulted Tombs of Mesara*, by S. Xanthoudides (University Press of Liverpool, Ltd.), for fig. 28; *Südwesteuropäische Megalithkultur*, by Wilke (Curt Kabitsch, Würzburg), for fig. 33 *a–c* and *e*; *Oldtidens Kunst Stenalderen*, by S. Müller (National Museum and the Royal Society of Northern Antiquaries, Copenhagen), for figs. 46, 47 *b*, 48, and 49; *The Proceedings of the Society of Antiquaries of Scotland*, vol. xxxvii (Society of Antiquaries of Scotland), for fig. 56; *Explorations in Turkestan*, vol. i, by R. Pumpelly, W. M. Davis, R. W. Pumpelly, and E. Huntingdon (Carnegie Institution of Washington), for figs. 65 and 66; *Mitt. der Anthrop. Ges. in Wien*, vol. l (Vienna im selbstverlag der Gesellschaft), for fig. 14 *d–e*; *Ephemeris Arch.*, 1908 (Société archéologique d'Athènes), for fig. 31 *a*; *Scotland in Pagan Times—the Bronze and Stone Ages*, by J. Anderson (Douglas & Foulis, Edinburgh), for figs. 52 *c* and 57; *La Civilisation énéolithique dans la péninsule ibérique*, by Nils Åberg (Upsala, 1921), for figs. 2 *a–b*, 3, 22 *a*, *b* and *d*, 33 *d*, 34 *a* and *d*, 54 *a–b*; *Das nordische Kulturgebiet in Mitteleuropa während der jüngeren Steinzeit II*, by Nils Åberg (Upsala, 1918), for figs. 7, 8 *b*, 10 *a*; *The Pottery from the Long Barrow at West Kennet, Wilts.*, by M. E. Cunnington, for fig. 51 *a*; and *Arch. Camb.*, vol. 80 (1925), pt. i, for fig. 53 *e*.

August 1929.   H. J. E. P. & H. J. F.

CONTENTS

LIST OF ILLUSTRATIONS

I

The Awakening of the West

IN the last volume of this series, *The Steppe and the Sown*, the story of civilization was carried on until the first signs of a settled existence had appeared on the threshold of western Europe. In chapter 5 of that volume we traced the movement of peasants, possessing the knowledge of agriculture, of pottery, and of domesticated animals, from the Danube basin, and perhaps from the border of the Russian steppe, until they came almost within sight of the North Sea, noting that on their route they kept closely to patches where the soil is that formed upon loess. In chapter 10, also, we pointed out that there must have been communications between the eastern and western Mediterranean in the days when corbelled tombs were used in Crete, when the Cyclades were passing through their second early phase of culture, and while the second city, probably in its second phase, was flourishing at Hissarlik. It is our view that these eastern influences upon the West continued for some little time, and that certain trade-routes along the Mediterranean, first suggested twenty years ago by Peet and more recently discussed by Frankfort, played an important part in these movements. Recent increase in our knowledge of these remote times makes it highly probable that the Second City of Hissarlik was a centre of great commercial importance, especially during its second phase, which we are inclined to date during the centuries following 2400 B.C.

At some period, probably rather before the date just mentioned, villages grew up at the head of the Gulf of Corinth, and the culture of these settlements was reinforced by Thessalians, who brought thither the pottery known as Dhimini ware, and by people from the Cyclades, who had landed earlier on the Plain of Argolis. From the head of the Gulf of Corinth a culture, containing mixed elements, spread to the island of Levkas, where cists have yielded considerable evidence of Cycladic and other connexions. Beyond that there were links with Molfetta and Matera in south-east Italy, and across that peninsula towards Sorrento and the island of Capri; besides that we have

FIG. 1. *Sese* in Pantelleria and *Nuraghe* in Sardinia.

evidence of connexions with south-east Sicily, in the regions around Syracuse, and some hint of relations with Malta. In the latter island the great stone monuments of elaborate design are important as suggesting connexion with a civilization possessing well-developed architectural ideas. The nature of the soft limestone in the south-east of Sicily seems to have led to the use of excavated vaults rather than of built-up tombs, while the *Sesi* found in the little island of Pantelleria, the *Nuraghi* of Sardinia and the *Talayots* of the Balearic Islands, seem related, though not very closely, for they are all circular structures of dry walling although different in their purposes.

The connexions farther west are best illustrated by the corbelled, built-up tombs of southern Spain, too closely related to those of Crete to be of independent origin, and possibly by the excavated grottoes found in western Portugal and elsewhere in the peninsula. It has often been thought that these corbelled tombs are the latest and most developed forms of the great stone monuments found in such numbers in the Iberian peninsula. We are inclined to think that this view is mistaken, and we shall argue for an alternative hypothesis, suggesting that the corbelled tombs and the west Portuguese grottoes were the chief indications of the awakening of the West by contact with the East.

There are, however, other evidences of such contact. An

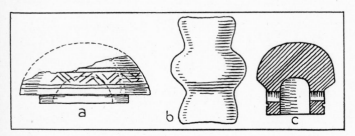

Fig. 2. *a.* Ivory knob from Nora; *b.* Segmented stone bead from Palmella; *c.* Ivory bead from Hissarlik.

ivory knob found at Nora in Portugal is in any case a remarkable object in view of the material of which it is made, but its resemblance to the ivory bead in Treasure Hoard L of Hissarlik II, which belongs to the third phase of that city, argues for a connexion with that place; a segmented stone bead, found at Palmella in Portugal, suggests links with the second phase of Early Cycladic culture.

Beads and ornaments of a material called callais have been found in great numbers in Portugal, all associated with the tombs of the dawn of the age of metal. Miss L. F. Chitty has estimated that about 1,000 such beads have been found in Portugal, while upwards of 700 have also been discovered in Brittany. The source of this material is unknown, but it is believed to be somewhere in the West. In the eastern Mediterranean twenty-seven beads, which appear to be of the same

material, have been found at Kadi Keui on the shores of the
Sea of Marmora. Though we cannot be sure, there is a probability that the eastern and western material may be from the
same source. When one adds to this the fact that several of
the pottery forms, found associated with the civilization of the
megalithic tombs in the Iberian peninsula, resemble those that
occur in the eastern Mediterranean, one feels that there is
ground for the view that there were connexions between these
two regions. The hypothesis, that this occurred by a westward
flow of commerce from Early Minoan Crete, from Hissarlik II
and from the Cyclades, by way of the Gulf of Corinth and
Levkas, is very attractive to hold, pending the gathering of
further evidence, for we know that the early inhabitants of Crete
and the Cyclades were active in maritime trade.

What human organization there was in Spain, prior to this
awakening under eastern influences, seems best pictured by supposing that the Capsian culture of east Spain continued, with
what are called Tardenoisian flints, and that the inhabitants
were still in the hunting stage. We think it probable, though not
yet fully established nor accepted by all the local archaeologists,
for example Bosch-Gimpera, that the Capsians did not of themselves discover the art of grain-growing nor how to make pottery, but acquired the rudiments of these arts from immigrants
or traders, who had landed in south-east Spain, in south-west
Portugal, and perhaps in Andalusia as well. In other words we
think the builders of corbelled tombs and the excavators of
grottoes probably introduced the elements of civilization, and
in a later chapter we shall develop a re-interpretation of the
Iberian dolmens and gallery tombs with their apparently early
furniture, based upon this supposition.

Some archaeologists have suggested that pottery, agriculture,
and megalithic constructions evolved in Spain, in the first
instance at least, independently of influences from the eastern

Mediterranean, while others believe that similar developments, equally independent of the Near East, took place in the Baltic region. Western Europe was, however, lacking in effective native species of grain-bearing plants, and grain cultivation is at the base of the structure of Old World civilizations; it is unlikely that grain should have been carried from its early home near the east end of the Mediterranean without being accompanied by elements of the civilizations associated with it in the Near East. Moreover, it is difficult to understand resemblances between the megalithic civilizations of the Iberian peninsula, Brittany, the British Isles, and the Baltic lands, without thinking of a connexion between them all, or of some intercommunication between various regions along the Atlantic shores. If such intercommunication existed, it is surely difficult to picture it utterly without links with the contemporary and largely maritime civilizations of Crete and the Cyclades. The stories of the Odyssey and of the Voyage of the Argonauts at least suggest that accounts of long voyages to regions of mystery far away from the Aegean were a feature of very early Greek tradition.

We do not think that the evidence available points to a complete transplantation of any one east Mediterranean culture; it seems rather to be a case of influences, probably from more than one ultimate source, rousing a population hitherto in a lowly condition, such as that described in the closing paragraphs of *Hunters and Artists*, the second volume of this series, a condition conveniently named epipalaeolithic. As the able students of prehistory at Liége have long insisted, the use of pygmy flints seems to have continued for a very long time, and it is only with the advent of polished stone implements, fine chipping for arrow-heads, and even metal, that the use of these flints declined.

An old-established use of the term Neolithic is to denote the period during which polished or ground stone was the material used for the best implements, before metal was introduced. There was once a tendency to look upon the Neolithic period, defined in this sense, as one of immense duration in most parts of the world, but the growth of knowledge has made it evident that the problem must be considered separately for different regions. It has become fairly clear that in Mesopotamia the art of stone-grinding may not be appreciably older than the early stages of metallurgy, both being practised at a very remote date. In Egypt stone-grinding is unknown save in the Badarian culture. For the spread of metallurgical arts both organization and means of communication had to develop, and, as it was only when bronze came into use that metal was found really superior to stone for most types of implements, it was until then to a large extent an article of luxury. It would seem that for this reason the art of metallurgy spread more slowly than that of polishing and grinding stone. It is even possible that some of the people of the north-west of Europe, while still in an epipalaeolithic condition, had discovered that a stone hoe, slightly ground at the edge, was more efficient for digging up roots than one not so ground; if so, we can readily understand that the practice of polishing such implements, together with the art of making pots, which are more useful vessels than baskets or leathern bags, may have spread rapidly, while the knowledge of metallurgy lagged behind. In other words it seems to us that the Neolithic Age of west Europe, with its polished stone implements, is essentially a phase heralding the advent of metal, and is related to a civilization which in its earlier home knew both copper and gold. That the neolithic phase may have lingered on in an island like Britain, or in a region rich in flint but poor in metal like Denmark, seems highly probable; this does not mean, however, that contact had not been made, though perhaps indirectly, with metal-using civilizations.

The modern climate in north-west Europe is generally considered to be favourable to the growth of initiative, as its conditions allow us to disperse a good deal of heat and so to work hard; many of us also have sensitive skins, which, combined with the high degree of energy, contribute to a highly sensitized nervous system. All this, so important for the development of a civilization, could not begin to have an influence until the Ice Age had long passed away; moreover it is only one factor. Along with it one must have an assured and plentiful supply of food for a settled population, as well as means of intercourse. The former was lacking until grain was brought in from the lands beyond the eastern Mediterranean; the latter does not appear to have developed to any considerable extent until the grain growers had become well established. As we have already pointed out in previous volumes, the effect of intercourse in weakening tabus and so in liberating initiative is a most important factor in the evolution of human society. It is our view that this liberation began in west Europe during the neolithic phase, the herald of metal culture, and that thenceforward this part of the Continent began to advance towards the high place in the world that the relation of man to climate makes possible for it.

Of the factors that contributed to bring about the awakening at this particular time we have already suggested a few. The spread of peasant life step by step from the south-east, in a period when the climate was improving in the north-west, explains itself, for the more assured mode of life is likely to displace the poorer, if climatic conditions are favourable. The spread of conquering lords from the steppe borders over the peasant communities seems to have been a marked event, which has repeated itself at intervals since. The difficulties of the last days of Sumer and of the Old Kingdoms in Egypt engaged our attention at the end of volume v, and they seem to show us that there was great activity among the people of the steppe and its borders, an activity that we can well appreciate when we realize that a warm and favourable climate in west and north-west Europe is likely to mean drought in the steppes; we must remember, too, that it was about this time that the horse first appeared in Mesopotamia.

In tracing the migrations of culture by land we must note the distribution of soils derived from loess and related material, for these are our main guides. Cultivation is easier on such soils, and Gradmann has well emphasized their importance from time

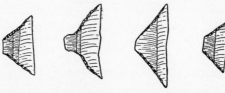

Fig. 3. Tardenoisian or late Capsian flint implements from Solsona, Spain.

immemorial as sites of settlement. The heavy clays, on the other hand, covered as they were with dense woodland, have usually been occupied at a later date and for a long time formed belts of difficulty, isolating early communities from one another, save in so far as waterways provided a means of transit. As regards sea movements we may remember that little enough can have been possible before the use of the wedge had become established by the sea-side, and that this had to be supplemented by some device for pegging or nailing together the planks before a boat of any size could be available. That this step should have occurred as copper was coming into use and becoming a material to be sought for is thus quite natural.

Having briefly surveyed these general ideas and postponed to the next chapter the discussion of the corbelled tombs and their contents, we may proceed to a short relation of the various objects found, especially pottery and polished stone, that seem to indicate the spread of elementary ideas of civilization. In east Spain the Late Capsian culture, with its art and its Tardenoisian flints, lingered on for a time unchanged, and it was a population in this stage of culture that seems to have learned

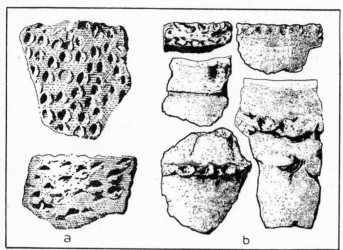

FIG. 4. Fragments of pottery with finger-tip ornament from: *a*. Spain; *b*. Southern France.

about pottery and stone-grinding from intercourse with people arriving from the East on the Almerian coast. The early stage of the new development was attended by a spread of improved equipment into central Spain, where Bosch-Gimpera finds a culture characterized by the use of hard rock of many kinds (such as basalt, schist, and limestone) for implements that are often very little ground or polished, by the persistent use of small flint chips and by the possession of a rough pottery ornamented with finger-tip impressions and nail grooves. Bosch-Gimpera associates with this culture some objects found at Murcielagos, which, in agreement with Åberg, we think are later. He also thinks that this pottery is an autonomous development; without much evidence to settle the question one way or the other, we are inclined to doubt this, and find it easier to think of pot-making as an art learned by backward folk from immigrants settled in all probability in Almeria. Of the cultural links between this rude civilization in east Spain and a similar culture in the south of France we think, with Bosch-Gimpera, there can be little doubt, and since similar rough pottery, with finger-tip impressions and nail grooves, has been found with neolithic associations on many sites in north Italy, in the provinces of Cuneo, Cremona, and Verona, we may picture this civilization as spreading in a region extending between Andalusia, southern France, and the basin of the Po, while before the close of the Bronze Age it had reached the neighbourhood of Taranto. We can trace this rough pottery culture of east-central Spain through France as far north as the department of Ardèche, and it seems provisionally justifiable to link up with it the rough pottery, associated with rather more numerous flint implements, that comes from Savigny and Saint Saturnin in Savoie.

It seems probable that to this culture we must ascribe some rock engravings found in the Ligurian Alps. Though many of these may belong to a slightly later date, when tools and weapons of bronze had come into general use, others seem to have been drawn, if we may judge from the forms of the implements depicted, when copper only was known. Somewhat similar rock engravings, believed to be of neolithic date, have been found in some parts of Spain, where they are thought to be degenerate descendants of the rock paintings of the Upper Palaeolithic period. It seems probable, therefore, that these rock engravings of the Ligurian Alps belong to the same culture, even though they be somewhat later in date.

Reinerth believes that the oldest pottery found in the Swiss lake-dwellings is that which he has termed *westische Keramik*; he notes its great poverty of ornament, so that it, again, may be related to the same source. One of the present writers has recently emphasized the relationship of this rough ware to the

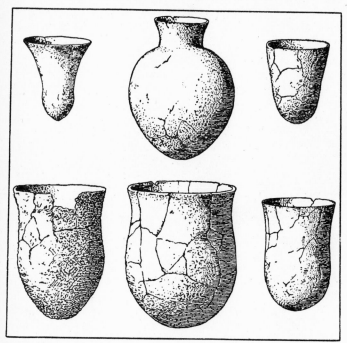

FIG. 5. Pottery from Michelsberg.

oldest pottery found in England, at Windmill Hill in Wiltshire. From Michelsberg in Baden comes a series of pots, well known to archaeologists, including 'tulip vases', which are considered by Reinerth to be a later development of this *westische Keramik*. This Michelsberg pottery has no parallels in England, but the earthworks of Michelsberg, and still more so those of Mayen in the Eifel and Urmitz by the Rhine, suggest connexions with those now being excavated at Windmill Hill.

As we interpret the evidence, this early western civilization developed considerably in the lands on either side of the Rhine, and the typical settlement is at Michelsberg, on a hill projecting into the Rhine plain near Untergrombach in Baden. Here was a settlement surrounded by a rampart of earth, pierced by numerous entrances. It is situated on a loess soil and was supplied apparently with water from a number of springs, one of which remains. The form of the earthwork closely resembles that now being excavated at Windmill Hill, but the pottery is more developed, for the tulip vase does not occur on the English site. This may be due to some extent to the interplay of this early western culture on the Rhine with peasant cultures of Danubian origin that had reached there from the south-east, and there are elements of kinship in pottery between this and other early settlements in central Europe. The Michelsberg culture occurs at many sites near the Rhine between Lake Constance and Cologne, a zone reached and actually crossed in some places at an earlier date by the Danubian peasants from the south-east, as we have mentioned in chapter 5 of *The Steppe and the Sown*. The Michelsberg settlements were those of grain cultivators, for remains of barley and wheat (more accurately emmer) have been found in round-based undecorated vessels shaped like a bell; such vessels, when they have developed a flat base and certain other features, are called 'beakers', and will be more fully described in chapter 3. The occurrence of emmer, both here and in La Hesbaye in Belgium, is interesting, since this form of wheat seems to have spread via the Mediterranean, whereas the grain used by the Danubians was einkorn at first and afterwards bread wheat. The people of the Michelsberg culture also had domesticated animals, including the ox, sheep, goat, pig, and dog; horse bones have been found among their remains, but these may have been hunted for food as were the deer and the fox. Their pottery includes, besides the bell-shaped vessels and the finely made but usually undecorated tulip vases already mentioned, some flat-bottomed bowls, shaped like truncated cones, some handled jugs with necks, a few dishes, and what are called 'sauce-boats'. Reinerth has recently shown that this culture has had a considerable influence on the civilization of the Swiss lake-dwellings.

There seems good reason for believing that the Michelsberg culture influenced some of the civilizations farther east. In the last volume of this series we described some early settlements of the Danubian peasants on patches of loess in the bay of lowland between the Harz Mountains and the Erzgebirge, the lowland on which Leipzig and Halle have grown up in later times. Of the early sites on this lowland, Rössen, described in chapter 5 of the last volume of this series, is the best known. Though the Rössen pottery is of finer material and more highly decorated than that of Michelsberg and belongs in a general way to the Danubian series, there have been found on the site a few more or less round-bottomed bell-shaped vases, which remind us of those from Michelsberg, as well as others that carry the same form raised on a well-shaped base or stand-ring. We do not think the time has yet come to be more precise about the inter-relations and relative chronology of the two cultures, but it does seem likely that at Rössen and elsewhere in the loess regions of central Europe there was to some extent a mingling of cultures.

We may sum up the general argument of this chapter by stating that the awakening of west Europe was due to intrusive influence from the east Mediterranean, first reaching east Spain, and carrying thither the ideas of pottery and grain cultivation. These ideas were then taken up by the epipalaeolithic hunters of the interior, and by them spread through France to Italy and the British Isles; also to Switzerland and southern Germany, where the new culture came into contact with the Danubian civilization, which had reached those parts some generations earlier. Other stages of this awakening will be dealt with in the following chapters, and throughout the volume we shall point out the interplay of influences from the Mediterranean through south-west Europe with those coming up the Danube from the south-east. Both sets of influences seem to have met and mingled in some of the loess regions of central Europe, the Rhine basin forming an early frontier zone between these two civilizations. We may add here, for the sake of those already somewhat familiar with the subject, that we believe the settlements at Campigny, Seine-Inférieure, and at the Camp de Chassey, Saône-et-Loire, both date from a slightly later time.

There is, however, a possible alternative to the theory we have propounded for the awakening of the West, namely that this culture reached Spain from north Africa. In chapter 4 of *Peasants and Potters* we described the Badarians and their culture, though we pointed out in the following chapter that, when we wrote, there was no evidence that these people cultivated grain. We also referred to the Fayûm culture, discovered by Miss Caton-Thompson, which we then believed to be much later in date. Early in 1928 Brunton announced that he had found grain in a pot in a Badarian grave, while Miss Caton-Thompson wrote that she had found evidence that the Fayûm culture preceded by a considerable time a Middle Predynastic settlement. It is clear from these discoveries that the Badarians were grain-growers, and that the Fayûm civilization is of approximately the same date. Since large stores of barley and emmer were found in the Fayûm deposits, it is reasonable to assume that the Badarians were acquainted with these grains.

We suggested, as Petrie had done before, that these Badarians were new arrivals from Asia, and this view has since received fresh confirmation. Miss Stoessiger has made a careful examina-

tion of sixty skulls of these people, and she finds that in form
these are intermediate between those of the predynastic Egyptians and of 'Dravidians and Kolarians', who are believed to be
remnants of the earlier peoples of India. Moreover the earliest
predynastic skulls most nearly resemble them, while those of
later periods diverge more widely. Childe has pointed out that
the culture of the earliest predynastic Egyptians shows affinities
to that of the Final Capsians of the Sahara, and cites the
evidence adduced by E. S. Thomas that on the black-topped and
white cross-lined pottery occur at least thirty signs that are
found on the walls of the rock-shelters in south-east Spain.
Flamand and Obermaier have also shown that certain decora-
tive features found in the rock-carvings in north-east Africa
occur also on the white cross-lined pottery. From this Childe
infers that the earliest predynastic people came from some part
of Africa north of the Sahara and west of the Gulf of Tripoli,
like the Final Capsian invaders of Spain. We think these movements may be related to the drying of the Sahara, which, we
believe, had a fair amount of rain during the Ice Age.

The Badarians and the people of the Fayûm used arrow-
heads with barbs but no tang and therefore with a concave base;
these we imagine were brought from Asia, for they do not occur
elsewhere in Africa until a later date. Still, such arrow-heads
have been found in Mauretania, in 'dolmenic tombs', and in
'neolithic' deposits in Algeria and Tunisia, and they are the
typical arrow-heads of the culture of the Iberian peninsula in
the early ages of metal.

It is clear that about the time that eastern traders were reaching the western Mediterranean, or conceivably some centuries
earlier, elements of civilization had been passing across north
Africa from Egypt to Morocco, eventually reaching the Iberian
peninsula. Whether these elements were carried by grain-
growing peoples or only by hunters is for the moment uncer-

tain, for as yet we have in north Africa no evidence of agriculture that can be attributed to so early a date, while the only pottery so far found consists of a few fragments, discovered by Reygasse at Redeyef in Tunisia, and these may well be later in date.

FIG. 6. Tulip-shaped vase of Badarian date from Egypt.

Some years ago Petrie bought in Egypt a beaker-shaped pot of black incised ware, which he figured as N. 58 in his Corpus of Prehistoric Pottery. Similar pots have lately been found by Brunton in association with undoubted Badarian remains. Childe has recently suggested that such pots may have given rise to the beakers which occur in Spain and central Europe, and which will be described in the third chapter of this volume. These Badarian pots seem to us to resemble the tulip-shaped pots of the Michelsberg culture, which we shall describe in the

next chapter, more closely than the typical beakers, and we suspect that the forms of both have been derived from leather
vessels used by the north African peoples. Some connexion between the cultures of north Africa and Spain seems probable,
but it is by no means clear that agriculture and the potter's art
were brought to the West by this route.

BOOKS

CHILDE, V. GORDON. *The Dawn of European Civilization* (London, 1925).
FRANKFORT, H. *Studies in the Early Pottery of the Near East*, vol. ii (London,
1927).

2

The Peasants of Central Europe

IN the previous volume of this series we traced the movements of
the Danubian peasants down to about the year 2200 B.C., when
we found them occupying, not only the whole of the Danube
basin, but much of the loess region north of the Carpathians
from Galicia to Thuringia, while advance guards had reached
the Rhine, crossing it at many places between Worms and
Cologne. We have noted, too, that many of them had settled
in Belgium, in the region around Liége known as La Hesbaye,
while one of their settlements has recently been discovered just
over the border of Holland. Others had reached Switzerland,
and had there erected pile-dwellings in the marshes around the
lakes, thus inaugurating the civilization of the Swiss lake-dwellings. Though a few slight traces of their culture, dating in all
probability from a rather later time, have been found in
France, the spread of the Danubian culture seems to have been
checked at the Rhine or just west of that river. What we have
learned in the previous chapter will explain this, for it must
have been about this time that the civilization, with its grain-
growing and rough pottery, which had started in central Spain,

was reaching the eastern parts of what is now French territory. We thus see, about the year 2200 B.C., Europe divided into several rather clear-cut cultural divisions. The Danubians stretched from the Iron Gate to the Rhine and just beyond, where they met the western civilization that had come from Spain. The Black Earth Lands seem for the moment almost deserted, the grass-lands of South Russia still held remnants of the nomads with their battle-axes, while civilization had barely penetrated to the North and the shores of the Baltic.

We have seen, too, that there is reason for believing that about 2600 B.C. some of the nomad, battle-axe folk from the grass-lands destroyed the villages of the grain-growers upon the Black Earth Lands and spread out in many directions, conquering and often destroying as they went. Some of these, we believe, entered the plain of Hungary, where they made themselves lords over the peasant communities, inaugurating the Second Danubian civilization. These seem to have followed the advancing peasants, at any rate as far as the Rhine, doubtless lording it over them there in the same manner as they had done farther east. Others went north into the forest lands around the Upper Volga, while others again seem to have spread to the north-west, some occupying eastern Galicia and the Ukraine, while others spread over north-east Germany, and perhaps reached the south-eastern corner of the Baltic. The opening of the Third Danubian period, about 2200 B.C., witnessed, it would seem, further movements of these masterful nomads.

In the Danube basin the peasants continued their former life without much change, and the line of traffic to the Erzgebirge, mentioned in the previous volume, followed by traders from Hissarlik, continued until the fall of that city about 1900 B.C. But the war-lords of the Danubian area were not left in undisputed possession of their territory.

We have seen reason for suspecting that during the general

exodus from the grass-lands about 2600 B.C., some of the nomads with their battle-axes entered the loess regions in the eastern end of Galicia. Rather before 2200 B.C. these, reinforced apparently by others from the grass-lands or from the forests to the north, pressed on through the open patches of West Galicia into Silesia, and we find their cord-ornamented pottery and flint axes lying above remains of the Second Danubian period at Jordansmühl. In one grave here, distinguished from its fellows by being surrounded by a ring of stones, there were found a number of relics of these invaders, a collared flask, a funnel-necked beaker, and two amber rings, lying beside a typical Danubian pot. At Nosswitz a new settlement with rectangular houses, believed to have been erected by the new-comers, lay above the remains of First Danubian huts. This invasion, as far as we can see from this evidence, had begun before the close of the Second Danubian period, which came to an end, we believe, about 2200 B.C. It was the spread of these people with their battle-axes over nearly the whole of the Danubian region that ushered in the Third Danubian period.

The invaders pressed on westward into Saxony and thence up the Elbe into Bohemia, and, judging by the occurrence of a number of polygonal battle-axes, they spread thence to Bavaria, while others of the group passed into Moravia, where their remains have been found on the hill of Stary Zamek. Wherever they went we find fresh elements of culture appearing. While doubtless they lived to some extent on the grain grown for them by the Danubian peasants, they occupied themselves much with hunting, and used many implements of bone. They did not have shoe-last celts, which the Danubians used for hoes, but stone or flint celts with flat faces and rectangular cross-sections, used probably as axes, while they adorned themselves with necklaces of bored teeth and clay beads instead of the *Spondylus* shells worn by the peasants. Their numbers were reinforced after a time by others, who almost certainly came from the northern forests, and may well have been the aboriginal inhabitants of those parts, with elements of civilization derived from the nomads of the grass-lands; these used cord-ornamented pottery and buried their dead under barrows.

In the second chapter of the previous volume we suggested that some people allied to the nomads of the Russian steppe had

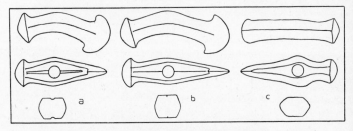

FIG. 7. Polygonal battle-axes from: *a.* and *b.* Bohemia; *c.* Bavaria.

moved into the park-lands that form the northern fringe of the grass-lands, and that these had mixed with epipalaeolithic hunters from the forests that lie still farther to the north, and had introduced to them the arts of grain-growing and pot-making. These spread to the north-west, through the forest lands of Poland and north Germany, making and using a type of pottery, decorated with impressions of cords, and known as cord-ornamented ware.

During the period under review these people had spread over most of the country between the Vistula and the Elbe, and had reached the shores of the Baltic in Pomerania. They used globular amphorae with decorated necks, below which were small loops for suspension, and tall flasks with raised collars at the bases of the necks. These, and other forms, were decorated with cord impressions. Their principal weapon was the perforated battle-axe of stone. They were scattered throughout central and eastern Germany, as well as through Poland, but by the beginning of this period those living in Thuringia seem to have become dominant. They buried their dead under barrows in a pit or a small stone cist, and the skeletons found there show them to have been tall with long and relatively narrow heads. Their chief weapon was the stone battle-axe, shaped with many facets; they possessed also spheroid mace-heads and occasionally

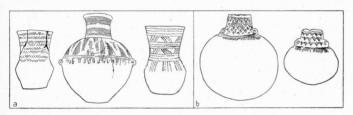

FIG. 8. Cord-ornamented pots and globular amphorae.

arrow-points or lance-heads of flint. For ornament they wore bored teeth and sometimes small coils of copper wire, as well as beads of amber and bone. Since no settlements of these people have been found, Schliz has suggested that they had established themselves as overlords over the Danubian peasants.

In the last chapter we suggested that the pottery, called by Reinerth the *westische Keramik*, was introduced from France into Switzerland, where it arrived, we believe, about 2200 B.C., and here this culture developed into that known as Michelsberg, with its tulip-shaped vases, about a century later. This Michelsberg culture gradually dominated the Swiss lake-dwellings, especially in the north-east, around Lake Constance. Thence it seems to have spread down from the Rhine, where its people at first lived in pile-dwellings by the river-side, or on platforms of logs laid on the moor, as at Weiher, near Schaffhausen. Soon, however, they took to living on fortified hills, and their camps can be recognized by the presence of two or three concentric

lines of ditches and banks, each pierced by numerous entrances, fortified with palisades of upright posts. The houses,
which were usually rectangular and sometimes sunk in the earth,
were arranged within the ramparts in regular streets. The dead
were buried in a contracted position, in a pit under the dwell-
ings they had occupied, which were then destroyed. The
greater number of the skulls of these people were long and

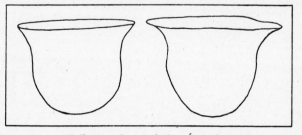

Fig. 9. Tulip vases from Boitsfort-Étang in Belgium.

narrow, but the occasional presence of a broader specimen shows
us that they had sometimes intermarried with the Danubians,
who had preceded them in this region. They used implements
made of bone and horn, their pottery was fine, often black or
grey in colour, and usually took forms suggestive of leathern
prototypes. They cultivated grain and used flat disks of clay,
upon which they baked their bread.

The centre of their civilization was on the Rhine, where
during this period they displaced many of the Danubian
peasants, as was the case at Goldburg, where their wooden
houses were found above the older pit-dwellings, containing
pottery of the Rössen type. In some cases, however, as at Flom-
born, the peasants remained comparatively undisturbed. The
Michelsberg people spread down the Rhine almost to its mouth,
and a settlement containing tulip vases has been found at
Boitsfort-Étang in Belgium.

We must now return to the people from the forest, who arrived through Galicia into Moravia. The spreading of these people seems to have continued until about 2100 B.C., or even later, but they do not appear to have made much headway in Hungary, where the earlier war-lords seem to have been able to hold their own, and were growing rich out of the trade between Hissarlik and the Erzgebirge. Meanwhile, before 2000 B.C., the Michelsberg folk began to pour down the Inn valley into

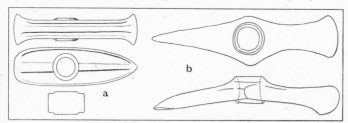

FIG. 10. Battle-axes with tubular projections in: *a*. Stone from Lehe, Hanover; *b*. Copper from Hungary.

Austria, and succeeded in penetrating Bavaria, Bohemia, and possibly Moravia. These, too, were kept at bay by the war-lords of the Hungarian plain. The latter were, however, attacked with greater success from the other side, though probably at a later date.

It has been pointed out that about this time there was introduced into Hungary and Yugoslavia a large number of copper battle-axes, which seem from their shape to have been brought from south Russia or the regions beyond. It is, of course, possible that these came in by way of trade, perhaps from Hissarlik, but most authorities believe that their presence indicates the arrival of a fresh group of invaders from the grass-lands. Childe hints that these people arrived early in the period under review, while Nagy believes that the invasion in question took place many centuries later, quite late in the Bronze Age. As we shall see later on in this volume, there are reasons for suspecting that unsettled conditions prevailed in the steppes and deserts round about 1900 B.C., and we are inclined to think that, if there were any new arrivals in Hungary from the East, it is to that date that we must refer them.

Double axes of copper had been introduced into Hungary by the first invaders at the beginning of the Second Danubian period, and had for long been made locally, especially in east Hungary and Transylvania. It was customary to punch the hole for the haft through the metal while still hot, and this left around the socket a tubular projection, which is sometimes found reproduced in stone battle-axes. The new copper axes, introduced as we believe about 1900 B.C., were of a different form, with single and not double blades, in many ways resembling a modern hatchet.

In spite of all these invasions the humble Danubian peasants continued much as before, tilling the soil with their shoe-last celts in much the same manner, whoever their lords might be. Bracelets of *Spondylus* shell are found in their graves alongside of copper implements, and even at a far later date, when bronze was well known, we find them making pottery and figurines in much the same way as before.

It would seem that it is to about this period that we must date the second series of settlements that grew up on the Black Earth Lands of south-west Russia. It will be remembered that a number of these had existed in Transylvania, Moldavia, and the Ukraine at an early date, but had been destroyed by the nomad people of the steppe about 2600 B.C. For a time the sites were abandoned, and in Transylvania they seem never to have been reoccupied. At Cucuteni, however, a new village arose in course of time on the old site, and the same was the case at Tripolje, near Kiev, while a number of new villages arose at the eastern end of Galicia. The pottery of the second settlements was very similar to that found in the earlier villages, for the most part painted, though more often decorated with incised ornament in the Ukraine. The people in the latter region seem to have had intercourse with Turkistan, for the skull of a camel was found in one of these settlements. Though copper tools were found in the earlier settlements, these are much rarer in

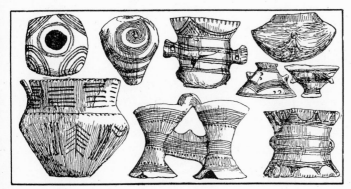

Fig. 11. Vases from Tripolje, near Kiev.

those of the later period, but a flat dagger was found at Bilcze Złota in Galicia. Other settlements of this period have been found at Koszyłowce, Kapuściuće, Czortoviec, Wygnanka, Wasylkowce in Galicia, and Schipenitz in Bukovina.

Until the fall of Hissarlik II the trade between that city and the Erzgebirge continued, and doubtless brought wealth to the Hungarian war-lords. Weapons and ornaments were introduced from the south-east, and copper daggers of Cypriote type have been found near Arad in Transylvania and at Stillfried in Lower Austria, while knot-headed pins of Aegean type have been discovered both in Hungary and Bohemia. The occurrence of bronze implements at Hissarlik during the last phase of the existence of the Second City shows that the traders from that place were familiar with the value of that alloy, but the entire absence of bronze objects in the Danubian area during the period throughout which this trade was going on suggests that the knowledge of this alloy was kept a trade secret and that copper was carried to the Aegean in the form of ingots and the tin as ore. Copper objects were produced in the Danubian region, though not in very great quantities while the trade with Hissarlik lasted. After the fall of that city, however, we find

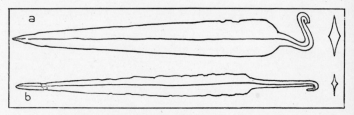

FIG 12.   Copper daggers of Cypriote type from: *a*. Cyprus; *b*. Aranya, in the gold-bearing region of Transylvania.

a considerable increase in native production, and the great influx of copper axe-heads from south Russia, probably from the north slopes of the Caucasus, may be in part due to the cessation of the Aegean trade.

It was, however, the inhabitants of Silesia, especially those living nearest to the Erzgebirge, that first made a speciality in the production of copper goods. These are found most frequently associated with a civilization known from the place where it was first noted as the Marschwitz culture. Marschwitz lies not far from Ohlau, a little town near the Oder, about twenty miles south-east of Breslau, but the culture extended considerably and later spread as far as eastern Moravia and Bohemia, and at a still later date occurs at Straubing in Bavaria. Graves containing objects belonging to the Marschwitz culture were found overlying deserted huts, belonging to the earlier half of this period, at Nosswitz. The interments, especially in Silesia, are in plain flat graves, in which the body has been placed in a contracted position, accompanied by fat-bellied jugs with handles, stone battle-axes with semicircular cross-sections, flint daggers made in imitation of copper weapons of west European type, and awls and rings of wire composed of a poor bronze containing little tin. Sometimes two, or even three, skeletons have been found in the same grave. The grave goods show us

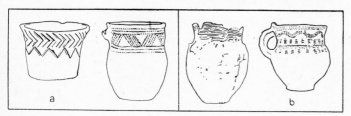

Fig. 13. Pottery from: *a*. Marschwitz, and *b*. Złota.

that by this time some trade connexion had been effected with Spain, and that the Marschwitz people had learned the art of mixing tin with copper, though they had not yet discovered the correct proportions or the value of the harder alloy for weapons and tools. The importance of this culture is that it laid the foundation of the Bronze Age civilization of central Europe, a civilization which, as we shall see in a succeeding volume, was destined to reach a high development.

Meanwhile civilization in Switzerland had not progressed but had rather been deteriorating, especially after the Michelsberg folk had moved eastwards and northwards. About 2000 B.C. some of the neolithic inhabitants of north Italy crossed the St. Bernard pass and introduced into the western region of Switzerland fresh elements of culture, such as have been found in the graves at Chamblandes, but these new elements were in no sense an advance on what was there before; the main development of the lake-civilization of Switzerland was yet to come. About 1900 B.C. the civilization in the Alpine region passed into its third or Upper Neolithic phase, but very little improvement is found except in the north-east. Here, in the lake-dwellings of Bavaria and Austria, the people came into contact with influences that had come up the Danube valley, and, especially at Mondsee, we find flat axes, riveted daggers, fish-hooks, and awls of copper, as well as double spiral ornaments of copper wire. The influence of the nomads from the northern forests is evident from the presence of polygonal battle-axes of stone, while the pottery improved and was decorated with deeply incised spiral motives, reminiscent of earlier Danubian ornament. A copper dagger, of Cypriote type, has been found in Canton Zürich.

The neolithic folk of north Italy continued to make rough pottery, decorated with finger-tip impressions, but about this time received by means of trade a few copper daggers. Some of these seem, from their form, to be derived from Cretan models, and probably arrived there from Sicily, but the majority appear to have come through Sardinia from Spain. One dagger of Cretan type was found with broad-headed skulls in a sepulchral cave at Monte Bradoni, which lies in the tin-bearing part of Etruria; this may explain the reasons that brought foreign traders to these parts.

BOOKS

CHILDE, V. GORDON. *The Dawn of European Civilization* (London, 1925).
BURKITT, M. C. *Our Early Ancestors* (Cambridge, 1926).

3
Great Stone Monuments

THE question whether any complex matter has ever been invented more than once has been much discussed. A great deal depends on the complexity of the matter and on its abstruseness or otherwise. Thus potters have at sundry times jested with the human features in decorating their handiwork; this is an idea that lies near at hand, and we should not, therefore, urge relationships between cultures merely on the ground of face decoration on pots, unless the style and the execution in two cases showed unmistakable resemblances. In much the same way it would be possible to argue that both communal burial and tombs built of great stones might arise, and arise contemporaneously, in two or more centres in complete independence of one another. When, however, we get communal burial, the use of great stones, and the high art of corbelling for a domed roof, all appearing with the dawn of metal culture in two Mediterranean regions, one at least of which had important maritime activities, we seem to be justified in thinking of a culture contact. In volume v of this series, chapter 10, and again in the first chapter of this volume, we have discussed the communal ossuaries of early Minoan Crete, noting especially the rectangular long-walled chambers at Mochlos and the corbelled tombs with fore-courts but no entrance corridors on the Mesara plain; we have also mentioned connexions between East and West, based on a few similarities in objects found in the tombs of the western Mediterranean, suggesting that these were evidences of culture contacts.

In this chapter we must take up the story at the western end, and may begin with the statement that the Iberian peninsula is very rich in communal graves or ossuaries, built with great stones; the contents of these have been used in arguments concerning their ages and origins. We will begin with a classificatory survey of types, ages, and contents as given by Obermaier.

1. Simple chamber dolmens, with uprights walling a chamber covered by a large slab. Contents: Ground stone axes of common materials, mostly of stout forms. Many flints. Simple points, harpoons, &c., of horn and bone. Simple pots of dish or beaker form, with slight decoration. A few personal ornaments, such as shells, bored teeth, and bone disks. Late Neolithic (14 *b*).

2. Chamber dolmens, with indications of a passage, walled by upright stones and covered by one or more slabs. Contents: Finer flints than in *a*, ornaments of *Pectunculus* shells, and a few 'idols' carved by incision in slate. End of Neolithic Age (14 *c*).

3. Chamber dolmens, with long entrance passages, often called gallery dolmens. The gallery or passage is roofed by a long succession of slabs. Contents: Axes of polished stone, often of rare materials from a distance. Highly retouched flint weapons, often with handles chipped, sometimes of dagger form. Pots finely ornamented with wavy lines, spirals, and geometric designs. The first bell-beakers. Beads of callais, 'idols' carved on slate slabs, amulets of animal phalanges. Some copper in the southern monuments (14 *d*).

4. Corbelled vaults, with or without entrance passages; also gallery dolmens and covered passages without a terminal chamber marked off. The corbelled vaults are often walled with small blocks. Contents: Polished stone axes of rare materials, evidently purely votive, wonderful daggers and other weapons of flint, arrow-heads, and many copper objects. Pottery of beaker type, with a little painted ware. Beads of gold, silver, and copper, gilded lead, ivory, amber in certain places, amethyst, turquoise, and callais. Arm-rings of ivory or stone. 'Idols' carved on slate palettes, or made from balls of limestone or alabaster. Richly

decorated or painted bone phalanges with figures of 'idols'. This is the Copper Age in the south of the Iberian peninsula.

5. Tombs with chambers and short galleries, or with small

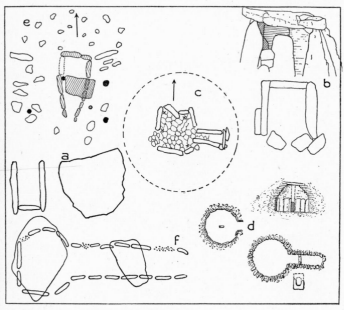

FIG. 14. Types of megalithic tombs in Spain: *a*. Stone cist at Otso-Pasage, Navarra; *b*. 'Simple dolmen' of Eguilaz; *c*. Chambered tomb with indication of passage at Cabecinha, near Cabo Mondego, Portugal; *d*. Corbelled vault at Gor, province of Granada; *e*. Chamber and short gallery, more or less fused into one, at Santa Cristina near Romanya de la Selva, province of Gerona; *f*. Chambered tomb with long passage at Cunha Baixa, Portugal.

cist-like chambers. Contents: Fine flint arrow-heads, often with stems. Much copper. Pottery for the most part simple, but a few beakers. Beads of stone and shell and ornaments of gold, silver, copper, and amber. Contemporary with *d*, but found only in north Spain (14 *e*).

6. Stone cists or boxes of stone. Contents: Few stone objects but many of copper and bronze. Metal harpoons, axes, daggers, rings, &c. Ornaments of gold, silver, and amber. Plain pottery. This culture is well marked in south-east Spain, where it is called that of El Argar, but it is widely distributed. It is generally agreed that these graves belong to the early part of the Bronze Age (14 *a*).

Obermaier gives interesting notes as to the methods probably used in the construction of the corbelled vaults and gallery dolmens. His classification has been accepted in principle by most of those who have studied the Spanish monuments, and some think, as indeed does Obermaier himself to some extent, that the simple dolmens are older than the corbelled tombs. We must admit that the parallel advance in monumental type and in the complexity of the contents is alluring; nevertheless we venture to think that this interpretation is incorrect.

In the first place we think, and in this we are in agreement with Obermaier and most other students, that the corbelled vaults in south Spain are a development of the same invention as the corbelled ossuaries near Mesara. In the southern half of the peninsula these tombs usually lie near the coast or at no great distance from it, though occasionally they are found farther inland; some are found also in north Portugal, between the Tagus and the Douro. If it be granted that the corbelled vaults, or to be more accurate the corbelling of communal tombs or ossuaries, embody an idea introduced from elsewhere, what can we say of the gallery dolmens, which occur with them though the latter are a dominant type farther from the coast? Do they represent a previous introduction, as their contents might lead us to suppose? If so, it is not easy to explain how they grade into or from the corbelled tombs, unless the two introduced cultures met and mixed, and this grading does not encourage that idea. If so, again, what is the origin of the gallery dolmen? Nothing found in the eastern Mediterranean, except in a very distant way the communal ossuaries of Mochlos, suggests the gallery dolmen; nor can an origin elsewhere be found, for the idea of the Danish monuments appears to be derived from that of the Iberian, rather than to have inspired it. Moreover, the culture-objects from the corbelled vaults and the gallery dolmens resemble one another too closely for us to believe that these monuments are widely separated in time or origin.

In general agreement with Le Rouzic, Childe and, we understand, also Daryll Forde, we venture to suggest that the corbelling, and the contents of such tombs, may represent the culture actually introduced, whereas lack of skilled labour or of mechanical resources led to the roofing of some chambers with slabs in the place of corbelled domes. In many cases, perhaps, the gallery dolmens, and still more the simple chamber dolmens, were put up by natives, acquainted with the introduced culture but possessing only slight skill in this type of building. On this view the dolmen of the simplest type may be no older, indeed would probably be later, than the corbelled tomb, and would stand in relation to it somewhat as a rural oratory may stand to a cathedral. In some cases a plain dolmen may be merely a simplification under stress of circumstances, whether due to rustic poverty or to other causes. The interpretation that we suggest does not conflict with the evidence furnished by the contents of the graves. The grave-goods at the great centres would clearly be of a more advanced type than those found in monuments erected by natives or by pioneers at far outposts, often living, as we have suggested, in remote rustic poverty.

On the whole the distribution of the monuments of 'simple' type, occurring as they do in a general way with greater frequency as one proceeds from the chief centres to the remoter inland parts, is in favour of our view. Nevertheless we would

3093.6   D

remind our readers that this interpretation is far from receiving general acceptance, and the balance of authority is somewhat against it, though few of the authorities really face the fact that corbelling, which passes gradually into slab roofing, or as some of them would urge is derived from it, must be an introduction from Crete, or conceivably from Libya whence Crete received that art. We would urge, too, that grotto tombs, sometimes

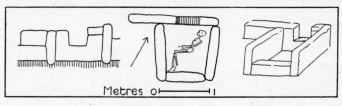

FIG. 15. So-called dolmen-grave at Monte Racello, Sicily.

constructed partly of large stones, such as occur as Los Millares in Almeria, at Monge near Cintra and at Palmella in west Portugal, are often approached by steeply descending passages; these cannot but be connected with the grotto tombs found in Sicily, Cyprus, and elsewhere.

The evidence taken as a whole seems, in our opinion, to favour the idea of culture contact rather than that of any extensive movement of peoples from any one of the centres of civilization in the eastern Mediterranean. It must, however, be frankly admitted that the evidence from the islands in the western Mediterranean does not give such clear indications of connexions from east to west as one might expect.

In some parts of Sicily there occurs a soft limestone rock, which can easily be cut with primitive tools, and here we find grotto tombs in abundance, often with more or less domed roofs. The tomb chambers, which were vaulted, were often approached by descending into a pit. In other cases a horizontal corridor or *dromos* was cut in the rock face; this corridor expanded into a chamber as soon as it got far enough into the hillside to avoid the danger of a fall of the rock lying over the chamber doorway. At Monte Racello in this island are graves hewn in the rock, which may, perhaps, be natural caves enlarged and remodelled. Side by side with these are graves built of slabs of stone. The latter contain only single burials and thus recall some Cycladic graves. These have, however, a special feature, for a square hole was cut out of one of the slabs near the top. This window has been thought to represent the doorway of the rock-cut tomb. Graves made of slabs are relatively rare in Sicily, where tombs cut in the live rock were more generally used.

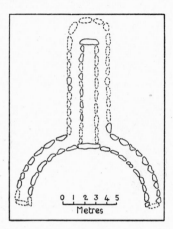

FIG. 16. Plan of a 'giant's grave' in Sardinia.

The presence of many rock-cut tombs in Sardinia shows that the culture of that island had connexions both with Sicily and with the Aegean, as is clear from the discovery there of the high-spouted pot or *Schnabelkanne* mentioned in chapter 10 of volume v. In Sardinia also there are large tombs, known as Giants' graves; these are built of great stones, and have fore-courts or entrance passages. It is interesting to note in passing that there is a monument in Ireland closely resembling these Sardinian tombs. Other early structures in Sardinia are the famous *nuraghi* or round towers; there are many of these in the island and they are believed to have been fortresses or refuges erected by the builders of the Giants' graves. These *nuraghi* seem to be related to the *Sesi*, graves found in the island of Pantelleria, which lies between Sicily and Tunis.

In Malta, again, we find some round buildings, of doubtful age it is true. The island is also famous for some most elaborate temples, made with large stones, such as those of Mnaidra,

FIG. 17. The Temple of Mnaidra in Malta. (By courtesy of British School at Rome.)

Hagiar Kim, and Hal Tarxien, as well as for the great underground structure or *Hypogeum*, with its domed vaults, cut out of the solid rock at Hal Saflieni. Round buildings, called *Talayots*, and circular tombs, which last Hemp has recently shown to have been cut in the solid rock, occur plentifully in the Balearic Islands.

In these islands of the western Mediterranean we thus find structures that we are inclined to look upon as evidence of the arrival of those influences from the East which aroused the West from its long slumber. In these islands, however, the ideas of monument-building seem to have undergone changes that resulted in the evolution of various types of monument in the different islands. One new feature, which is not to be found in the eastern Mediterranean until a later date, occurs with great frequency in the West. This is the corridor leading into the tomb, a feature which, it may be surmised, presented less difficulty to the builders than the corbelled vault. The corridor is found very generally among the elaborate monuments in the Iberian peninsula. When we consider the difficulties of good corbelling on a large scale, we can understand that a corridor would be added as an inevitable result, when a large mound had been erected over a relatively small corbelled vault.

We are of opinion that contacts of culture, brought about most probably in the first instance by sea, awoke the West from its epipalaeolithic condition. Thus the idea of communal tombs, or at any rate of ossuaries for the group, then current in parts of the eastern Mediterranean, spread to the West, where it expressed itself in diverse forms, according to the opportunities and difficulties of the various regions. We do not, therefore, think it profitable to attempt to construct a general classification of megalithic monuments, though there are resemblances between many of those occurring in the Iberian peninsula, the West of France, Ireland, and Denmark. In several regions, notably in Le Morbihan in Brittany, and in Wiltshire, megalithic constructions show special and distinctive elaboration, and in these places we have indications of an interplay of culture from various regions, suggesting that this interplay has, as usual, liberated initiative and led to special developments, very different in different cases.

If our view that the corbelled tombs are indications of an intrusive culture is correct, the much discussed question of the Neolithic or Copper Age date of the monuments becomes a matter of minor importance. We suggest that those responsible for the intrusive culture were at least beginning to be interested in metal, but we prefer not to speculate at the moment upon the possibility or otherwise of the intruders being engaged in a search for metal. It is significant enough, however, that south-east Spain has long been famous for metalliferous ores. Even if metal were known to some extent, the art of metallurgy may not have spread very rapidly, since for many purposes copper, at any rate, was no improvement upon stone. It may well be that the art of polishing stone may have spread first, and indeed we cannot be sure that it had not already reached western Europe, in advance of the Danubian peasants, before megalithic structures began to be erected in those parts.

The problem of the great stone structures is complicated by the fact that monuments, believed to be related, though distantly, to those of western Europe, occur in south Russia, the Caucasus, Palestine, Transjordania and elsewhere in the Near East. We venture to think that these monuments are best interpreted as modifications of the cist or Cycladic tomb. A feature found in many of them is the aperture on one of the walling slabs; this is usually round and it has been thought that it was devised to allow the ingress and egress to the soul of the deceased. The typical grave, in south Russia and the Caucasus at least, seems to be rather that of a leader and his dependents than an ossuary of the *tholos* type of Crete. The great grave at Maikop, described in chapter 2 of the previous volume, had a frame of wood, whereas others have one of stone, and it has been suggested that the wood-framed grave may have had a fairly wide distribution, especially in central Europe. It is difficult to test this speculation, and one might easily give it too much weight. It is at least significant that the idea of a 'port-hole' in the end slab is found in various cists, possibly of later date, in central Europe, and, as Kendrick points out, on the fringes of the megalithic province in Sweden and in a few cases in western Europe, including the cave-burials in the valley of the Marne. It seems, however, to be foreign to the Iberian and

Breton cultures of this time, though it occurs as an exception in a monument near Kerlescant in Brittany, and a somewhat similar feature occurs also in a dolmen-like tomb at Monte Racello in Sicily. Did the culture of the Copper Age in south Russia and the Caucasus spread its influence across the Continent to its western shores and carry with it the port-hole idea, to be applied here and there in the tombs, whether megalithic as in the case of Kerlescant or rock-cut as in some cases in the Paris basin? This seems possible, but cannot be said to be established.

On the whole, then, we think that, looking round the fringes of the ancient civilizations, under which we include Mesopotamia, Egypt, Cyprus, Crete, the Cyclades, and Hissarlik II, it is possible to infer the spread of various ideas concerning tombs and burial rites. Among these we may enumerate the idea of the Cycladic grave, primarily a cist with a single burial, the custom of burying attendants in or around a leader's tomb, such as has recently been found at Ur and Kish in Mesopotamia and of which vestiges occur in Egypt, and the idea of an ossuary or communal tomb of which we have an example on the Mesara plain in Crete. Or, if we consider the structures rather than the customs, we note the spread of the cist graves, the corbelled vault, the cave, enlarged or not, the rock-cut tomb, with or without an entrance passage or shaft. Within the regions of the old civilizations slabs or dry walling might be used. Around its fringes slabs were not always to be found, nor was there always the skill for dry walling and corbelling. Excavation in the live rock was practised in several cases where circumstances permitted. Elsewhere, as we think, a certain impressiveness, that could not otherwise be obtained for lack of skill in architecture, was secured by the use of large blocks of stone for side walls and for roofs in the place of dry walling and corbelling. The Great Stone Monuments of the West may, therefore, be looked upon as a kind of developed 'Colonial' style, if this term may be used without implying that colonies had been planted in the places concerned. It seems to us that a certain intertwining of Cycladic and Cretan features is noticeable in the tombs of the West, while the other monuments of great stones found in western Europe, such as Stonehenge and the alignments at Carnac, seem to be special developments that are not to be traced back to any closely related prototypes in the eastern Mediterranean. In south Russia and elsewhere in the Near East, on the other hand, we are inclined to see the interplay of Cycladic and Mesopotamian cultures, or of cultures related to these, which we may or may not be in a position to describe in the future, as investigations in Anatolia proceed.

It seems to us that one of the features, forming part of the intellectual equipment of the higher civilizations of the east Mediterranean and the riverine lands of the Near East, was a belief in immortality, of a more developed kind than had hitherto been found in the West. This belief was a natural accompaniment of civilizations in which the ideas of duration and continuity had grown to a remarkable extent. The practical value of a belief in immortality has shown itself in human society in many ways, while it exhibits many and diverse forms of development. As the exploration of monuments of antiquity progresses, it may become possible to say more about the form of that belief in the civilization that intruded itself into the West in the early days of metal culture. That it had some connexion with the idea of ossuaries seems probable.

While fully corbelled tombs exist in the Iberian peninsula, they are found elsewhere in the West at this period only at Île Longue in the Morbihan, at New Grange in Ireland and at Maes Howe in Orkney; the last of these may be later in date. There are, however, indications of partial corbelling at Le Moustoir near Carnac in Brittany, at La Hougue Bie in Jersey, at Capel Garmon in north Wales, and in the Danish island of

Zealand; moreover, this list is probably incomplete, and Forde
thinks there may have been corbelling at Rosmeur in the Breton
department of Finistère. These instances seem to show that the
builders of these monuments were acquainted with an art practised rarely because of its difficulty.

Fig. 18. Ceremonial pillar in Cave 14 near St. Eugenie in Mallorca.

As to the methods of building with great stones, we think
the views of Obermaier are probably correct, and so summarize
them briefly. He believes that, in the erection of a gallery-
dolmen, the roofing stones were first laid in order on a suitable
mound. Then the soil was dug out from beneath them, while
their ends were still left supported upon the undisturbed earth
at the sides of the chamber and corridor thus formed. Subse-
quently the walls, both of the chamber and of the corridor,
were faced with stone, either with small stones laid as a dry

wall, or with large standing stones as in the more typical megalithic monuments.

Another view is that a trench was dug in the ground for the corridor, the sides of which were lined with vertical stones or dry walling. Then the roofing slabs were placed in position with their ends supported partly by the untouched earth at the sides. Pillars were sometimes placed in the chamber to give additional support to the roof, but some occur that appear never to have reached the roof and seem to have had only a ceremonial purpose. Such pillars have been noted by Hemp both in Wales and in the Balearic Islands.

The corbelled tomb may have been built over a solid mound of earth, which was afterwards removed. The chamber thus made would afterwards have been covered with earth, partly for protection and partly to increase the size of the monument. The erection of a large monument meant either extraordinary skill in corbelling, which we believe to have been rare, or the construction of a passage through the superimposed earth into the corbelled chamber. The erection of a large monument would, therefore, necessitate the laborious construction of a long corridor, if the chamber remained accurately in the centre of the mound. When difficulties were experienced in building a corbelled dome, the custom arose, so we believe, of roofing the chamber as well as the corridor with large slabs. In some cases a further modification was the shortening of the corridor by placing the chamber nearer to the entrance.

BOOKS

CHILDE, V. GORDON. *The Dawn of European Civilization* (London, 1925).
KENDRICK, T. D. *The Axe Age* (London, 1925).
PEET, T. ERIC. *The Stone and Bronze Ages in Italy and Sicily* (Oxford, 1909).
PEET, T. ERIC. *Rough Stone Monuments and their Builders* (London, 1912).
FERGUSSON, JAMES. *Rude Stone Monuments in all Countries* (London, 1872).

4

Beakers and their Interpretation

FORMS of pots, known as beakers or drinking-cups, and belonging to the dawn of the metal age, are found, sometimes associated with other pottery, in central Europe, the British Isles, the Iberian peninsula, south-east France, and Brittany. The *Glockenbecher* or Bell-beaker of central Europe and the Iberian peninsula is of a broad bell shape with an almost flat base. The sides of the bell have the typical constriction at the centre, sometimes fairly sharp, though at other times with a graceful curve; this constriction divides the somewhat bulbous lower part from the neck, which in form resembles a truncated cone with the wider end forming the rim. A decoration of zigzags, or horizontal or vertical lines, sometimes in patches alternating with others left plain, is usually arranged in horizontal zones around the pot, and has been incised, sometimes by a comb or a toothed wheel. By further development complex patterns have been obtained.

Bell-beakers differ considerably among themselves in the proportion of their diameters to their heights, and it would seem that those with flat bottoms and relatively small diameters are commoner in central Europe than in the Iberian peninsula. In Britain the beakers are taller and narrower, while their necks have an almost cylindrical form. Here, too, and in central Europe as well, one finds beakers ornamented by impressions of cords, usually in horizontal lines; this indicates the influence of the *Schnurkeramik* or corded-ware upon this particular type of vessel. This type of decoration, with a slightly different technique, is found occasionally in Spain.

The beakers of central Europe and of Spain are far too much

alike in general style to be considered separate inventions.
They are elaborate vessels, by no means the work of rude
beginners. The original home and the evolution of this form,

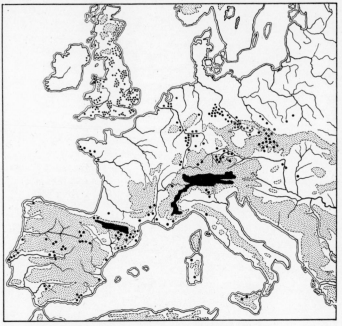

FIG. 19. Map showing the distribution of beakers.

as well as the interpretation of its distribution, have occupied
the attention of many minds.

A widespread opinion, due in the first instance to Hubert
Schmidt and recently championed by Bosch-Gimpera and A. del
Castillo Yurrita, is that the form of this pot and its decoration
originated in the south centre of Spain; the last writer has
elaborated, and somewhat modified, this point of view. He
thinks the bell-beaker in the valley of the Guadalquivir is

a natural continuation of the incised pottery of the caves of Andalusia, and he considers that the ornament of the latter foreshadows that of the bell-beakers. In other words he looks

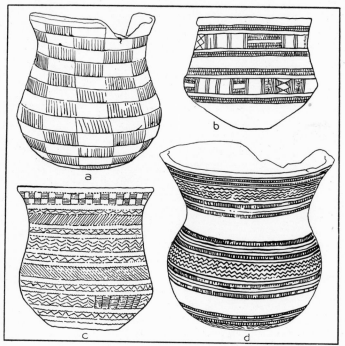

FIG. 20. Typical beakers from Spain and central Europe: *a*. San Isidro, south-central Spain; *b*. Wanzleben, Saxony; *c*. Bylany, Czechoslovakia; *d*. Ciempozuelos, south-central Spain.

upon the cave pottery of Spain as mainly indigenous, with possible influences from Almeria or north Africa. In this we cannot think that he is right, for we feel convinced that the potter's art was most probably an introduction. On the other hand he is of the opinion that it was the mingling of this indigenous culture with a number of exotic elements that gave rise to the bell-beaker culture in the Guadalquivir basin.

We admit the possibility of this general idea, but do not think it as yet sufficiently established that the cave civilization is anterior in time to that of the beakers, for to argue purely from typology to chronology is always a risky process. In our opinion it is worth while, at this stage of the growth of knowledge, to

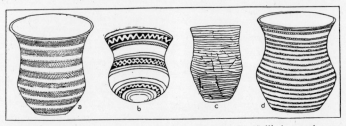

FIG. 21. Zoned and cord-ornamented beakers: *a.* La Halliade, south-west France; *b.* Bitterfeld, Saxony; *c.* Summertown, Oxford; *d.* La Halliade, south-west France.

have one or two alternative hypotheses, which we shall venture to suggest in due course.

Related to the beakers are dishes, usually shallow and shaped like parts of the surface of a sphere; these are very specially Iberian. They have continuous lines or rows of points as their decoration, and a typical scheme gives radial lines, often forming a four-armed cross, on the rounded bottom, with lines parallel to the circumference towards the rim.

Before considering the evidence from central Europe, we should mention the beakers found in other west Mediterranean lands, about which no dispute arises. They have been found in the Balearic Islands, and they occur with the shallow sphere-sectioned dishes in Sardinia, at Anghelu Ruju, Cuguttu, and San Bartolomeo; a few have been found in Sicily, at Villafrati, and Carini, while fragments have been reported from Gerace and Puleri. A cave in the province of Lucca in north Italy has yielded fragments that seem to be related to beaker pottery,

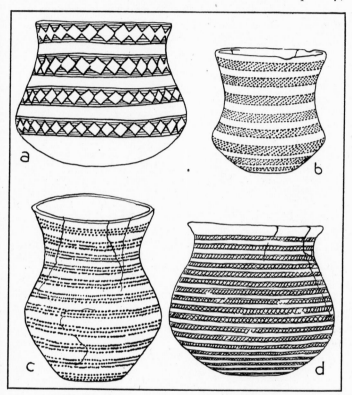

FIG. 22. Bell-beakers from: *a.* Anghelu Ruju in Sardinia; *b.* Villafrati, Sicily; *c.* Ca' di Marco, north Italy; *d.* Santa Cristina, north Italy.

while elaborate beakers have been discovered at three sites in the province of Brescia, the best known of which is Remedello. In all these cases, as is generally agreed, we seem to have instances of a spread *from* rather than *to* Spain, and in chapter 1 we have already suggested that the rough *westische Keramik* spread from east Spain to other lands, notably to north Italy. Everywhere in the islands, but less definitely in north Italy, the beakers appear to be intrusions into the local cultures.

Returning from this Mediterranean excursion, we must next note that the beaker is common to Spain and the lower basin of

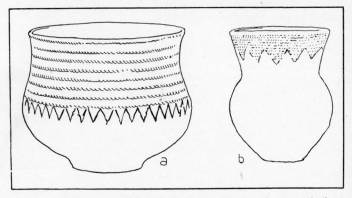

FIG. 23. Beakers from east-central Europe: *a*. Brusno, Cieszanow district; *b*. Ksiaznice Wielkie, Pinczow district, Poland.

the Rhône, while it has been found fairly frequently under the southern slope of the eastern Pyrenees, though there it is an intrusive element. Bosch-Gimpera considers that these beakers of north-east Spain were borrowed from the central Spanish culture, though he says that they seem to have been the only borrowing that occurred. He also says that the beaker style of decoration spread from that region beyond the beaker area, and that one can trace its degeneration as it spreads. With this last point we are in full agreement. Later on we shall suggest that it is possible to think of central or east-central Europe as the original home of the beaker. In that case the places where it occurs in south France, north-east and central Spain may be interpreted as stations on routes between central Europe and southern Spain. We mention this idea here, so as to bring an alternative picture before the reader's mind.

We must now turn to central Europe, where the beaker is known from about a hundred sites or groups of sites. Though the beakers of central Europe have usually, as we have already stated, relatively flat bases, a few occur with the rounded base on which the four-armed cross decoration is occasionally found.

Beakers have been found here and there along the Rhine from Lake Constance to the neighbourhood of Cologne; they are specially abundant in the Rhine Palatinate. The other main groups that have been found were in Bavaria, Moravia, Silesia, Bohemia, and the Elbe-Saale region near Halle and Leipzig; there have been outlying finds in Hungary. We note, however, the following, which come from farther east; some are beakers, others have merely the general shape of the bell-beaker and decoration related to that of the wares of the Black Earth region.

1. A beaker from Złota, Poland.
2. A beaker from Ksiaznice Wielkie.

Both of these are rather high in proportion to their diameters and have not the true form of bell-beakers.

3. A cup with a conical base from Koszyłowce near Lemberg.
4. A rough pot from Gatnoë near Kiev.
5. A broad pot from Jackowice near Kiev.
6. Painted, bell-shaped pots from Horodnica in Poland and from Transylvania.

When one considers the shapes current among the pots in the settlements of the Michelsberg culture and some of the forms and decorations of the vessels of the Rössen type, both of which have been found in what later became beaker regions, one is much tempted to think of a hypothesis alternative to that of Schmidt, and to look upon the beaker as a standardization, in both form and decoration, of various types of pots used in a number of central European cultures, that seem to have been not completely isolated from one another. We note in the first place that these cultures belong to the zone of the loess, from the earliest times a zone of intercommunication as well as of settlement, both because it was less obstructed by forest than the areas of clay soils, and because the soil was of special agricultural value. In the second place beakers are found as objects associated with materials belonging to diverse cultures, but there do not seem to be in central Europe settlements of beaker-making people with a complete equipment of their own. Beakers have usually been found in graves with a few accompanying objects that might well be the equipment of a mobile group. Hence the theory has arisen that the Beaker People had considerable military prestige, and spread rapidly, rarely settling anywhere for long. This may be so, but, having regard to the links between the many local cultures of central Europe at that time, we should be inclined to be satisfied with a slightly more modest hypothesis. Before putting this forward we must mention several other regions in which beakers have been found.

It is generally agreed that a spread from the Rhine carried the beaker to Holland, where it is found in a definite area south and south-east of the Zuyder Zee, not far, yet nevertheless distinct, from the area of the great stone monuments in the province of Drenthe. Yet the two cultures effected exchanges, for some beaker pots have been found in the megalithic tombs.

Near the great megalithic areas of Denmark and the west Baltic one finds a culture, originally, it would seem, distinct from the megalithic, and characterized by single graves, i.e. graves originally made for individual interment. Beakers have been found in these, and, it seems, they underwent a special development in association with the single-grave culture of

Denmark. Dr. Sophus Müller and Dr. H. Kjaer consider that
this single-grave culture was an intrusion into Jutland from the

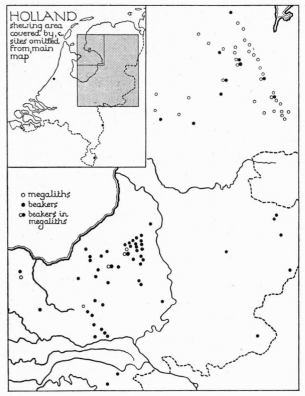

Fig. 24. Map showing distribution of beakers and of megaliths in Holland.

south. If so, we may assume that some beakers and related
objects found in certain megalithic tombs indicate that here,
as in Holland, the beaker and megalithic cultures came into
contact with one another.

E 2

More than four hundred beakers have been described as having been found in England and Wales, and, as the result of Dr. Fox's work, there seems no longer any doubt that their makers landed at various points along our east and perhaps our south coasts. They spread thence to the west, where one finds, notably in Wiltshire but also to a slight extent elsewhere, indications of contacts between the beaker and megalithic cultures.

The beakers of Brittany and of south-west France have a very great interest, but we are inclined to think that they reached these regions through movements along the lines of connexion between the megalithic centres of the west. For this reason we omit them from this stage of the argument, and propose to discuss them later under their respective regions.

It will now be seen that we consider Spain to be in a position more or less analogous to that of Holland, Denmark, and Britain. We are inclined to think that the beaker culture stretched out from central Europe to connect with the megalithic culture in Almeria, Andalusia, and Portugal, as well as in Holland, Denmark, and Britain. In south-east France and north-east Spain the two cultures are much mingled.

Without indulging our imaginations so far as to suppose that there was some large-scaled organization, with commercial or governmental stations, along the land routes of Europe at the dawn of the metal age, we may be allowed to suggest that there was something tending, it may be only slightly, in this direction. Some continuity of cultural feeling must have existed between the beaker stations and some system of intercourse was arising.

Very few objects other than flints have been found with beakers in central Spain, but in central Europe one usually finds 'bracers' or, supposedly, wrist-guards of stone, triangular flint arrow-heads, with the stem and barbs of nearly equal length and parallel-edged in some places. In other regions the arrowhead is stemless and has the base concave between the barbs; small copper daggers with short stems also occur, as do polished stone axe-heads of rare materials, often with the butt-end pointed. These objects are typical of the earliest days of metal, and there seems, therefore, reason to associate the rise and spread

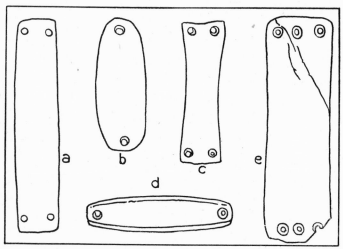

Fig. 25. Bracers from: *a*. Bylany, Czechoslovakia; *b*. Anghelu Ruju, Sardinia; *c*. Brescia, Italy; *d*. Carmona, Andalusia; *e*. Brandon, Suffolk.

of the beaker in central Europe with the last three or four centuries of the third millennium B.C., a period for the most part prior to the discovery of bronze, which discovery we think may be associated with the second city of Hissarlik during the third and last phase of its existence. Bracers have been found with the beakers in the Remedello culture of north Italy, and objects, possibly akin to bracers, occur with beakers in Brittany, but not on the central Spanish, Pyrenean, or south French sites. They do occur, however, in Andalusia, Almeria, and Sardinia.

The geographical gap between the south-east French and

the Rhenish beakers is mysterious, and it is noteworthy that much the same gap occurs in the distribution, as we interpret it, of the early western pottery described in chapter I. In both cases some instances occur in Savoy that need to be taken into account, but, in view of the difficult character of the country, this does not seem very helpful in the present stage of our ignorance. If we look upon the beakers as evidence of some kind of organization on routes in Europe, or as an expression of some aspect of the life of people concerned with trade along those routes, the fact of the big gap just noted is a little less difficult to understand than it would be if the beakers were supposed to represent the spread of a people, as it were step by step, by conquest or folk migration. It is well to remember, too, that the early lake-dwellers were occupying much of the intervening region, and may have acted as carriers for the beaker-folk.

We may draw attention to the fact that the beaker culture imparted an influence observable in the pottery technique of the various local cultures into which it intruded; in some of these the beaker designs show evidence of degeneration, as in the Pyrenean region and, for that matter, in Britain. Whether this degeneration occurred or not, the beaker culture decayed on the European continent as the knowledge of bronze spread early in the second millennium B.C., and soon afterwards vanished everywhere. This, to our mind, suggests that some organization or aspect of life, extending over large areas, was profoundly altered; doubtless bronze brought with it, in Europe at least, revolutions of power and of commercial intercourse, involving changes of centres and of trade routes.

A further point arises here that is at least interesting, even if it be but a coincidence. It was apparently about the time that Hissarlik II was reaching the height of its greatness with the rebuilding of its walls, roughly dated about 2200 B.C., that the beaker became important on the European loess. It declined soon after Hissarlik was destroyed, as Frankfort thinks, by Anatolian, probably Hittite, invaders. We must add that Hissarlik II seems to have had widespread interests, presumably of a commercial nature, in central Europe and throughout the Mediterranean, as we pointed out in chapter 2 of the preceding volume, *The Steppe and the Sown*, and of the present volume.

In our last volume the story of important parts of eastern Europe was shown to hinge upon the conquest of cultivable areas by steppe warriors, the men of the stone battle-axe. It may well be that some of these warriors retained to a certain extent their ancient mobility and power of organization, a power which, we cannot but think, became of commercial rather than of military importance. In conjunction with local influences here and there they may have developed the beaker culture, which seems to us to belong primarily to the loess regions of central Europe. The skeletons found in association with objects belonging to the beaker culture, especially on the loess, include long-headed men, who might well be related to the warriors of the battle-axe. In west-central Europe and the west, on the other hand, and notably in Britain, are found broad-headed men of very strong build with powerful brow-ridges, the origin of whom Keith thought years ago could be traced back to Polish Galicia. Given the apparently biological dominance of broad-head over long-head in parts, at least, of Europe, it is possible that the beaker-men of the west represent the original stock, with its tall powerful build, strong face, and prominent brows, modified by the increase of head breadth, appearing as the result of an admixture of stocks.

Farther than this we do not wish to go at present, save to remark that, when we come to megalithic monuments and beakers in our survey of the archaeology of Europe, we are no longer dealing, as in earlier times, mainly with local or even regional life; we are in the presence of cultural features that hint at what may already claim to be European systems. Occupation of the loess areas and the coastal entries is well marked; we have, apparently, the beginning in many regions of a tradition that has been more or less continuous from that time to ours, however its origins may have become obscured through play of fancy in the meanwhile.

BOOKS

ABERCROMBY, THE HON. JOHN. *Bronze Age Pottery* (Oxford, 1912).
CHILDE, V. GORDON. *The Dawn of European Civilization* (London, 1925).

5

The Merchants of the Aegean

WE have already shown, both in *The Steppe and the Sown* and in the earlier chapters of this volume, that a considerable trade existed between the Aegean region and the western Mediterranean during the closing centuries of the third millennium B.C. Though this trade at first started from the head of the gulf of Corinth and carried wares made chiefly on the Greek mainland, there have been found in the west goods that seem to have come from Hissarlik and from Crete. Both these places doubtless grew rich as the result of this traffic, but, while the merchants of Hissarlik appear to have been content to allow their goods to be carried in foreign ships, the merchants of Crete, long accustomed to organize a maritime trade, seem to have sent their fleets direct to Sicily and to other lands in the west.

The geographical position of Crete lent itself readily to this trade, for the island lies almost equidistant from Egypt, Hissarlik, and Cyprus, and is but little farther from Sicily and the north coast of Syria, while the Cyclades and the mainlands of Greece and Asia Minor lie still closer. In addition, the Cretans had long been accustomed to the use and manufacture of copper goods and had been still longer acquainted with the potter's art, for civilization had appeared here earlier than in

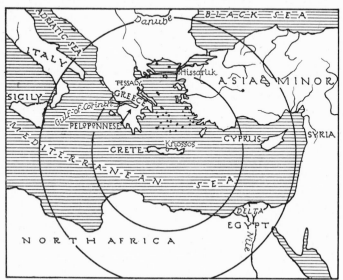

FIG. 26. Map of the eastern Mediterranean, showing the central position of Crete.

any other European region. It is small wonder, therefore, that, as this western trade developed, Crete should claim a full share.

During the unsettled times, described in the last volume, through which the kingdom of Egypt had been passing, trade with the Nile valley had been at a standstill, and little better opportunities for commercial dealings had been offered by the states on the mainland of Asia, which were also experiencing a series of crises. Meanwhile the people of Hissarlik had been developing an overland trade with central Europe, obtaining gold from Transylvania and copper from Hungary; later on they had found the latter metal, and tin as well, in the Erzgebirge. At the same time the Cycladic folk, who had settled in the Peloponnese, had opened up a lucrative trade with the far west.

In 2160 B.C., as we shall see in a subsequent chapter, settled government appeared again in Egypt with the establishment of the Eleventh Dynasty, and trade relations were renewed between Crete and the Nile valley. Hissarlik had grown rich and its exports were increasing, but its merchants appear not to have been shipowners. Here was a chance for the maritime traders of Crete, and they seem to have seized upon the opportunity of the revival of Egyptian trade to open up fresh communications with Hissarlik and to inaugurate a trade with Sicily and other western lands, including the province afterwards known as Etruria, rich as it was in copper and even tin.

The most convenient port for the Egyptian trade was at Komo, near Dibaki, in the Bay of Mesara on the south of the island, where the refugees from the Delta had landed more than a thousand years before. The best port for Hissarlik was near Candia, just to the north of Mesara, and both of these were nearer to the west than the earlier centres of Cretan civilization at the east end of the island. At the beginning of the Middle Minoan period, which following Evans we date at about 2100 B.C., not long after the rise of the Eleventh Dynasty in Egypt, there was a general shifting of the population from the eastern end to the centre of the island. A flourishing settlement arose at Phaestos in the south, and the former village in the north at Knossos increased in importance, while a well-made road connected these two centres. On the summit of Mount Júktas, which rises in comparative isolation beside the valley through which this highroad ran, there was erected a sanctuary, surrounded by a wall of cyclopean masonry, afterwards considered to be the tomb of the Cretan Zeus. The eastern centres became gradually depopulated, though Gournia, near which there were deposits of copper, continued to flourish for a while.

Fig. 27. Polychrome ware from Palaikastro, of Middle Minoan I date.

It was this shifting of the population, and the increased wealth that accompanied it, that ushered in the First Middle Minoan period; many changes accompanied it, especially in the types of pottery produced. A tower or keep, with deep-walled cells, in a more or less square area enclosed with massive walls, was erected at Knossos, while a building of rather less imposing appearance arose at Phaestos. Many houses were built at this time, usually with a rectangular plan, though an oval building of this date has been uncovered at Chamaezi. Various sanctuaries were erected, at which were offered votive figurines of terra-cotta, representing human beings and animals.

The pottery, often in the form of jugs with handles, was usually of a buff colour, decorated in dark brown; a common design on this was the so-called 'butterfly' pattern, which may have represented a double axe. Some of the pottery of this time was very thin, the so-called egg-shell ware, decorated with white designs on a dark glazed slip; this developed into a polychrome ware, better known from the site at which it was first discovered as Kamares ware, in which the vases are decorated in white and vermilion on a dark ground, in white, orange, and vermilion on a black glazed ground, or in some of these colours on a ground of pale buff or deep red glaze. On many of the vases of this period are representations of fishes, birds, goats, flowers, or foliage.

Some of the vases take shapes more suitable for metal, and even have on their surfaces imitations of rivet-heads. From this it has been inferred that cups and other vessels were often made of precious metals, more probably of silver than of gold. A silver vase of this date was discovered at Gournia. The silver was probably obtained from Hissarlik, near which several rich deposits of this metal occur, and it is hardly a coincidence that many of the cups, made in imitation of those of metal, are of the Kantharos type, with two high handles, a form very common at Hissarlik since the foundation of the Second City.

The copper implements were of much the same form as had existed in earlier periods, but the intercourse with Hissarlik had introduced into the island the knowledge of bronze, which now tended to supplant the softer metal. A hoard found at Chamaezi included double axes, an axe-adze of typically Cretan form though derived from one long used in Mesopotamia, and

long chisels resembling those found at Hissarlik. In an annex
to the smaller tholos at Hagia Triada were found a number of
riveted daggers, some of which contained more than 9 per cent.
of tin.

A number of figurines give us some idea of the costume of
this period. The men wore little but a waist-cloth, into which

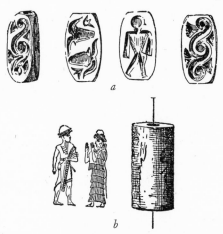

FIG. 28. Seals from Crete: *a*. Cretan seal engraved with signs;
b. Babylonian seal from Platanos, Crete.

was thrust a short dagger, and occasionally a small disk-like
cap. The women wore a skirt and girdle, with a bodice open
at the breast and rising behind into a high 'Medici' collar; on
their heads they wore hats with the brim expanding in front.
Three-sided seals, often of steatite, and semicylindrical seals
of ivory, were used; some of these were imported from abroad,
and afford valuable evidence for dating the period. In a small
tholos ossuary at Platanos near Gortyna, Dr. Xanthoudides
found a cylinder seal of haematite that appears to have come
from Babylonia, and to date from the Third Dynasty of Ur,

2409 to 2328 B.C., and Minoan imitations of Egyptian scarabs, such as were used during the early part of the Twelfth Dynasty, which began about 2000 B.C. In a cave at Psychro was discovered an Egyptian scarab of amethyst, of a well-known Twelfth Dynasty type.

During this period the tholos, erected in earlier times, continued in use, though no more tombs of this kind were made. Such communal ossuaries gave way to family tombs or cists, as the inhabitants of the eastern end of the island, who were, we believe, of Cycladic origin, settled more in the centre. At Gournia there were rectangular tombs, built like houses, complete with doors. Even the custom of family cists began to disappear before the close of this period, and we find not infrequently single skeletons buried in a contracted position in large jars or in clay chests with lids.

After the rise of the Twelfth Dynasty about 2000 B.C. Egypt became more prosperous and trade with Crete increased to the great advantage of the islanders, so that some of the merchant princes grew rich. Some of these began to erect great palaces, which included workshops and storehouses, and seem also to have contained shrines, used not only by the princes but by their subjects. The two most famous palaces erected at this time, about 1975 B.C., were those at Phaestos and Knossos, the latter incorporating the tower already described, while a third, only slightly less important, was erected at Mallia a few miles to the east. The building of these palaces may be considered as bringing to a close the first half of this period, known shortly as M.M.Ia.

The state of civilization in Crete during the second half of this period does not differ materially from that of the first phase, except that the rulers of Knossos and Phaestos were evidently growing in wealth and power. Certain differences are observable in the pottery, but these are of too technical a nature to describe here. All through the period we have seals on which are engraved not only figures and scenes but also signs, that seem to imply the beginnings of a pictographic script or some form of picture writing.

About the year 1900 B.C., the date as we shall see of the fall of Hissarlik, and some time before the end of the Twelfth Dynasty in Egypt, the First Middle Minoan period gave place to the Second, though this change was effected without any violent catastrophe. The main evidence of change is a development in the style of the pottery; the polychrome wares become commoner and more elaborate in design, while dark decoration on a light ground begins to supplant the former custom of painting the ornament in light colours on a dark background. The increasing wealth of the lords of Knossos enabled them to add to their great palace, and, as late as the end of the Twelfth Egyptian Dynasty in 1788 B.C., the prosperity of Crete remained undiminished.

While prosperity in Crete was increasing it was declining in the Cyclades. The wealth of the island of Melos consisted in obsidian, which had been much in demand for the finer quality of tools when copper was scarce. As, however, this commodity became more readily accessible, and especially when bronze came into the market through the enterprise of the Hissarlik merchants, obsidian was no longer in demand, and the people of Melos fell on evil days. It is true that the more enterprising of their number had long left for the Peloponnese, and were now setting sail for the West from the head of the Gulf of Corinth, but those left in the islands had lost their trade, and their prosperity had been declining throughout the Third Early Cycladic period, which is considered to have lasted later than the corresponding Minoan phase. It is well on in the First Middle Minoan period that we find a change occurring in these islands. Fortresses were erected at Paros and Syros, possibly by Minoan merchants, and at the beginning of the Second Middle Minoan period the second city was erected at Phylakopi in Melos, probably as the result of a Minoan invasion. From that time on the fortunes of Crete and the Cyclades were in many respects alike.

The fortress standing at this time by the Dardanelles, on the site upon which Troy afterwards arose, was the second settlement upon this hill, and is known as the Second City of Hissarlik. Its brick walls were twice rebuilt, and thus there are three phases in its existence. With the two first phases we have dealt in our previous volume, and we must now turn to the third phase of that city, usually known as Hissarlik II c. When the walls were rebuilt for the second time is uncertain, but it cannot well have been before 2200 B.C., nor is it likely that the beginning of this third phase can be placed later than the opening of the Middle Minoan period, which took place, as we have seen, about 2100 B.C.

The merchants of Hissarlik were great rivals to those of Crete, but, whereas the traders of Knossos and Phaestos were mainly engaged in maritime trade, their contemporaries on the Dardanelles carried on much commerce by land. We have already had occasion to mention their activities in the Danube basin, where they were in touch with the copper mines of south-east Hungary, and perhaps with the rich goldfields of Transylvania. We have noted, too, that they had penetrated as far as the Erzgebirge, and had obtained in those mountains copper, and most probably tin as well. If this latter view is true, as Childe has with good reason suggested, we may attribute to the merchants of Hissarlik the discovery that the addition of about 10 per cent. of tin to copper produced an alloy, not only harder than either of the component metals, but also melting at a lower temperature. It is, at any rate, certain that bronze tools and weapons were found among the remains dating from the third phase of this city, and that these are the first bronze objects known, unless some found recently in Mesopotamia and in India turn out to be true bronze and of an earlier date. There is no doubt that the people of Hissarlik at this time had bronze in abundance, and that their workmen cast implements of this alloy is attested by the numerous moulds found in the deposits of this time. That they kept their knowledge secret, in order to retain their monopoly in this commodity, is likely enough, and to this we may trace the legends of the Cabiri, Dactyli, Curetes, Corybantes, and Cyclops, all of whom were reputed to have had great skill as metal workers in far distant times. Associations of smiths, protecting trade secrets, and living rather apart from the general population, are a widely used subject of legendary history.

The geographical position of the mound of Hissarlik doubt- less helped its owners in their commercial success. Not only were there rich deposits of silver in the mountains behind, but it was situated at a most convenient spot for intercourse between Europe and Asia. Besides that, it lay also within a few miles of the Dardanelles, the narrow channel leading from the Aegean region to the mouth of the Danube and the Black Earth Lands of south Russia. Mariners using this route with great difficulty, owing to contrary winds and the down-flowing current, would stay to obtain water at the mouth of the Scamander, which enters the Dardanelles close by. For such a privilege the men of Hissarlik could easily exact a toll, which could only be refused with difficulty.

Such a simple way of raising wealth may well have been copied elsewhere by the men of Hissarlik, and it is not surprising that suggestions have been made that they founded a colony at or near Chalcis in Euboea, on the banks of the Euripus, the channel with strange currents that separates Euboea from the mainland. It seems likely that this settlement may have been a few miles south-east of the present town, where a spring of fresh water, called Arethusa like many similar springs, rose close by the sea-shore, and it may be noted that a fort, with walls of rough polygonal masonry, known as Pelasgian or Cyclopean,

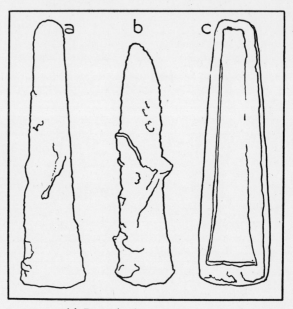

FIG. 29. *a* and *b*. Bronze implements, and *c*. Moulds for casting them, from Hissarlik.

lies on the summit of the hill overlooking the spring. The name of Chalcis, indicating some connexion with bronze, for which it was famous at a later date, may have some connexion with the bronze industry of this time. No suggestion has been made that they had other such colonies, but it is worth noting that at the southern mouth of the Bosphorus lay the city of Chalcedon, founded many years later by the men of Megara.

The site of Chalcedon closely resembles those of Chalcis and Hissarlik, its name indicates connexion with the bronze industry, while on its site now lies the little village of Kadi Keui, where recently were found those beads, thought to be of callais, to which reference was made in the first chapter.

The civilization of the third phase of Hissarlik II did not differ markedly from what had obtained there before, but there are considerable signs of increased wealth. Vessels of silver and gold were not uncommon, as well as personal ornaments of the same materials. The commonest objects, however, are tools and weapons of bronze, which leaves us in no doubt that the wealth of the city was mainly derived from dealings in this alloy.

At a date that is usually fixed at about 1900 B.C., the city was attacked and taken and its buildings burned. Who composed the attacking force is uncertain, but the discovery of two long-headed skulls with massive jaws, under conditions that led Schliemann to believe that they were the remains of the attackers rather than of the defenders of the city, suggests that the city fell before an assault led by some band of nomads from the south Russian steppe, whose activities at this time we have already suspected, though, in the opinion of Frankfort, these attackers were the Hittites. The city was not rebuilt for many centuries, and the humble villages which arose successively on the site are known as Hissarlik III, IV, and V.

About 2300 B.C. the civilization of Thessaly is considered to have passed into its third phase, during which the culture introduced at the beginning of the second phase declined. The painted ware, the distinguishing feature of the earlier phase, almost disappeared and was replaced by rough monochrome pots, and others decorated with geometric designs in white on a black or brown-black ground. Another ware made its appearance at this time. This, which is called crusted ware, is painted or crusted with a dusty white or pink paint, which readily came off when washed or rubbed. This ware occurs also at this time in the Danube basin, and its appearance in Thessaly may betoken fresh arrivals from the north, probably through the Vardar valley. In the eastern part of the country the pottery retained its former style, a survival of the First Thessalian ware, influenced

Fig. 30. Terra-cotta figurines with stone heads from Thessaly.

by the ribbon-ware of the Danube basin; here incised patterns, often including spirals, still continued. Though the pottery in the west degenerated in quality and decoration, the forms of the vases developed, and we find high-footed bowls, high-handled cups and goblets, hour-glass amphorae and jugs with cut-away necks. These new forms seem to have resulted from intercourse with the people of Hissarlik and the Cyclades.

The terra-cotta figurines, so common in earlier times, also degenerated in form until they became shapeless figures of clay, often with stone heads, on which the human features were painted. Finely polished stone celts became rarer, and their place was taken by a rather clumsy type of cylindrical form. Metal has been found only in small quantities, but it seems probable that implements of bronze were acquired by trade before the close of this period, which is usually dated 1800 B.C.

There is no perceptible break between the culture of this period and that of the preceding, yet Dr. Wace has suggested that a new people must have arrived in Thessaly. That there was anything like an invasion, such as ushered in the second period in eastern Thessaly, we much doubt, though it is probable that the presence of a fresh type of pottery, found in the lower part of the Spercheios basin, betokens the arrival of a new people. We are inclined to attribute the decline in civilization to the gradual departure of the more enterprising descendants of the invaders who had introduced Dhimini ware at the beginning of the second period. These had, before the close of that period, extended as far as the head of the Gulf of Corinth, where, in conjunction with Cycladic traders from Argolis, they had inaugurated a lucrative trade with the West. This trade, we imagine, attracted all the more energetic descendants of the Dhimini folk, leaving behind them in Thessaly the less progressive and the descendants of the earlier peasants. This would be a sufficient cause to account for the decline of the pottery and other elements of civilization, which we need not attribute, as Wace has done, to the introduction of the use of bronze.

Neither in central Greece nor in the Peloponnese was there much change until about 1900 B.C. Then occurred a great invasion of central Greece. The second city of Orchomenos was stormed and burned, and the invaders erected on the site a new town with rectangular houses. These newcomers buried their dead in a contracted position in cists or under fragments of large broken jars. They introduced a new type of pottery,

a hard well-turned silver-grey ware, known to archaeologists
as Minyan, though this must not be taken as implying that the
invaders were the people known to Greek tradition by that

FIG. 31. *a*. Jug, with butterfly decoration, from Drakhmani,
and *b*. Bowl of Minyan ware from Dhimini.

name. A tomb of one of these new people was found at Drakhmani in Phocis. Under a barrow was found a contracted
skeleton, accompanied by several monochrome Thessalian pots,
some Minyan ware and a matt painted jug with 'butterfly'
decoration of First Middle Minoan type, but which is believed
to be an importation from the Cyclades.

The origin of this Minyan ware was for some time in doubt,

for no pottery has been found elsewhere that can be considered as ancestral to it. Forsdyke at one time thought that it had been introduced from Hissarlik, but Childe pointed out that the Minyan ware from that site is some centuries later than that found at Orchomenos, and suggested that it developed in Phocis. Frankfort has more recently supported this suggestion, and believes that it developed from the plain black or dark grey ware in Phocis and Boeotia, as a result of the general advance due to the mingling of several distinct cultures in that area. He suggests that its silver-grey colour was due to the fact that it was made to imitate silver vessels, and points out that the forms found outside the region of its origin are without exception cups and goblets.

The identity of the destroyers of Orchomenos still remains a mystery. Childe suggests that they were northerners; this may be so, since there seems to have been some outpouring of the people of the steppe at this time. It seems likely, however, that these were the new arrivals in the Spercheios valley described on page 69. We find that cist burials with Minyan ware gradually spread from central Greece both northwards into Thessaly and southwards into the Peloponnese, and by 1800 B.C. the invaders seem to have made themselves masters of the whole of the eastern half, at any rate, of the mainland of Greece.

BOOKS

CHILDE, V. GORDON. *The Dawn of European Civilization* (London, 1925).

EVANS, A. *The Palace of Minos at Knossos, Crete* (London, 1921 and 1928).

GLOTZ, G. *The Aegean Civilization* (London, 1925).

FRANKFORT, H. *Studies in the Early Pottery of the Near East*, vol. ii (London, 1927).

LEAF, W. *Troy, a Study in Homeric Geography* (London, 1912).

LEAF, W. *Homer and History* (London, 1915).

SCHLIEMANN, H. *Ilios* (London, 1880).

SCHLIEMANN, H. *Troja* (London, 1884).

WACE AND THOMPSON. *Prehistoric Thessaly* (Cambridge, 1912).

6

The Iberian Peninsula and Southern France

THE high plateau of the Meseta forms a large part of the surface of Spain, and much of it is difficult country, so that the various coastal fringes of the Iberian peninsula, Portugal, Andalusia, Murcia, Valencia, and Catalonia, have usually been culturally very distinct, and Andalusia has repeatedly stood out. It did so already at the dawn of the age of metal. It held great possibilities for maritime communication, while it lay near the mineral veins at Huelva and elsewhere on the southern edge of the Meseta; moreover its rich soil and subtropical climate made it favourable for cultivation.

East of Andalusia lies Almeria, the mines of which gave it a leading position in the copper age; it is worth remembering that here Cartagena arose at a later date. On the west, below the steep edge of the Meseta, lay the coastal plain of Portugal, a region open to the sea, especially at the magnificent entry of the Tagus, while along the south coast there was the attraction of metal in the hills behind. To the north of Portugal lay Galicia, with lines of hills fringing out towards the sea and the Atlantic penetrating up the sunken valleys beneath them; its streams seem to have had metal-bearing sands, while its interior was difficult of access. The northern coastal plain beneath the Cantabrian Mountains with their mineral veins of many kinds is cut by many sunken valleys, and has a long tradition both of metallurgy and navigation. This plain stands out distinct from Navarre, which lies around the southern flank of the western Pyrenees.

In north-east Spain, Aragon in its hill-frame and Catalonia on the coast have each come to play a leading part since varied cultivation has developed. In early days it seems that it was the district on the south flank of the eastern Pyrenees that was of the greatest consequence. It may well be compared with the south flank of the western Pyrenees, for both seem to have been crossed by lines of transit joining France and Spain. The two

FIG. 32. Map of the Iberian peninsula.

regions have characteristic resemblances and differences, the eastern being richer in cultural remains of early periods, owing to its relations with Almeria, the Mediterranean coast of France, and the Balearic Islands.

We have already indicated our opinion that maritime communication through the Mediterranean, or just conceivably land communication across north Africa, brought to the Iberian peninsula the idea of the ossuary with a corbelled vault and its Mediterranean counterpart, the chamber sepulchre hollowed out of the rock. We must now add that these features may best be observed around four great centres; these are Almeria, the mouth of the Guadalquivir, Algarve on the south coast of Portugal, and the Tagus entry. Near these centres we find corbelled ossuaries containing some foreign goods, metal and numerous indications of external influences.

Many of these foreign goods we have already mentioned in our last volume, *The Steppe and the Sown*, or in the first chapter

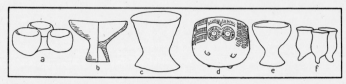

FIG. 33. Spanish pots of foreign types: Triplet pots from *a*. Almizaraque, Almeria, and *f*. Hissarlik; Vases on hollow feet from *e*. El Argar, Almeria, and *b*. Knossos, Crete; Vases on feet from *d*. Los Millares, Almeria, and *c*. Naqada, Egypt.

of this one. They include triplet pots, characteristic of several east Mediterranean lands, basins on a high, hollowed-out foot and bowls shaped like our modern sauce-boats. Then there is the ivory knob from Nora in Portugal, closely resembling an object from Treasure L from the third layer of Hissarlik II, 'idols' carved out of balls of limestone or alabaster, and a stone bead from Palmella, which seems to have Cycladic affinities. To these we must now add bone buttons with V-shaped perforations, found in Portugal, Catalonia, southern France, the Balearic Islands, Sardinia, Italy, and Greece, as well as in central Europe and in the Baltic region. We must mention, too, stone vessels, a feature of the eastern Mediterranean, and biconical or carinated pots, very characteristic of the Mediterranean region, as well as vessels with several short projecting feet on a more or less rounded base, though these may be late introductions into Spain. An interesting and important feature, found in Portugal and at Los Millares in Almeria, is a series of schist palettes, usually rectangular or trapezoid in shape, with a small hole for suspension near the middle of one edge. Similar objects

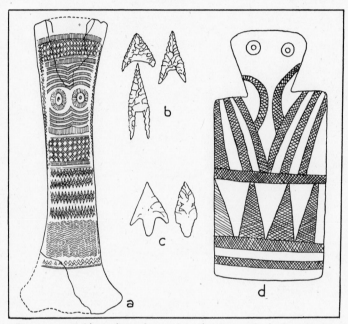

Fig. 34. *a.* Schist palette from Alemtejo, Portugal; *b.* Knuckle-bone figure from Almizaraque, Almeria; *c.* Flint arrow-heads with concave bases, and *d.* with stems.

have been found in Sardinia and south Italy as well as elsewhere in the Mediterranean. They seem to be prototypes, or more probably degenerate forms, of the figurines, usually female, widely distributed throughout all parts of the eastern Mediterranean except Egypt. Conventionalized representations of the human figure on knuckle-bones have also been found both in Almeria and in Portugal.

The richest tombs of the Iberian peninsula have produced flint daggers and arrow-heads of very fine workmanship, related to the best examples in north Africa and Egypt on the one hand and in Denmark on the other. Some of these flint weapons seem modelled on metal prototypes. The most characteristic arrow-heads from Iberian tombs have two barbs but no tang. This type occurs also in Ireland and Denmark, but is rare in Brittany, Britain, and central Europe, where tanged arrow-heads are the rule. The latter type is found also in south-east Spain and on the slopes of the eastern Pyrenees. Though flint-chipping reached such a high level, the art of stone-grinding was well developed, an art unknown in Egypt after Badarian times, and little known elsewhere in north Africa. Rare and choice stones were ground into axes that seem to have been used only as votive offerings.

Beads, an important feature, are of two materials, callais and amber. Callais beads have been found in tombs of the early metal age both in west Portugal and in Le Morbihan, Brittany, while amber beads have apparently not been found in either region, though claimed erroneously for Le Morbihan. On the other hand amber has been found both in the British Isles and in the Baltic area, while callais does not occur in either. There seem, then, to be two distinct provinces for amber and callais respectively; amber but not callais has been found in Finistère, Brittany. The two provinces overlap, however, in the south of the Iberian peninsula, for both materials have been found at Algarve in south Portugal and at Los Millares in Almeria; also in the Marne valley in France. Callais has been found in La Grotte des Fées near Arles and amber in a number of simple dolmens in the departments of Gard, Aveyron, Ariège, and Hérault. In the callais region of Portugal and south Spain rings have been found, made of choice stones like jadeite, as well as of ivory; some jadeite rings have also been discovered in Brittany.

The amber found in south Spain is clearly of foreign origin, though whether from the Baltic or not is uncertain; ivory is also an importation. In materials, therefore, as well as in styles of decoration, we have the clearest indications of maritime connexions for the civilization that was responsible for the corbelled tombs of southern Spain and the grottoes of west Portugal. It is believed that callais was found somewhere in

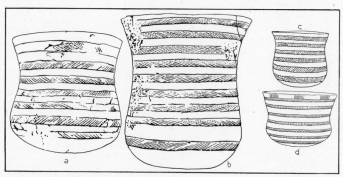

FIG. 35. Beakers from the west coast of Europe: *a*. Fuentes de Garcia Rodriguez, Galicia; *b*. Rosmeur, Finistère; *c*. Carnac, Le Morbihan; *d*. Palmella, Portugal.

the west, perhaps in Le Morbihan, perhaps in the Iberian peninsula. Whether this substance was native or of foreign origin, the occurrence of beads of this material at Kadi Keui near the Bosphorus shows us that it was a material used in maritime trade. Gold, in the form of rings, spirals, and diadems, and in thin leaves, has been found in the great corbelled tombs. The metal may be of local origin, but the forms are not very distinctive. A gold gorget from Cintra in Portugal, now in the British Museum, shows evidence of Irish workmanship, but this dates from a later period.

The objects found in the south-east of Spain differ in many respects from those found in Andalusia, and both show contrasts with the objects from west Portugal. This has led Bosch-Gimpera and others to define three cultural provinces, with perhaps south Portugal as a fourth. All of these, but Andalusia in particular, have yielded specimens of a particular kind of pottery, which includes the bell-beakers described in our fourth chapter, together with shallow bowls characteristically decorated on their rounded bottoms. These are clearly intrusions from central Spain into Almeria and west Portugal, but A. del Castillo Yurrita thinks that they evolved in Andalusia, as the result of the impact of a great immigrant civilization upon the native incised pottery of the caves. It seems to us, however, that the incised decoration of the cave pottery is more likely to be a crude imitation of that found on the beakers, which may quite possibly have originated in east-central Europe, and reached the megalithic area of Spain from that centre, as they did the similar areas in Britain, Holland, and Denmark.

If the beaker culture is of Andalusian origin, it is very singular that its distribution in the Iberian peninsula differs so profoundly from that of the megalithic culture. The former is found in central and north-east Spain, with a few examples in Galicia in the north-west; the latter seems to have spread inland from the coast, especially from south and west Portugal, degenerating as it went, so we think, from the corbelled tomb to the dolmen. The very slight influence of the megalithic culture upon New Castile on the arid Meseta, apart from its south-east corner, is an interesting feature; we think it suggests that the megalithic people were specially interested, at least during their earlier phases, in maritime trade and the cultivation of the land. The beaker culture, on the other hand, we have associated with land routes radiating to megalithic centres on or near the coast; if this be so, the south part of the Meseta would be an important centre for it. While the beaker culture, when in contact with the megalithic area of Andalusia, is part of a rich culture complex, on the Meseta these pots occur with very poor flint and stone weapons. This lack of cultural

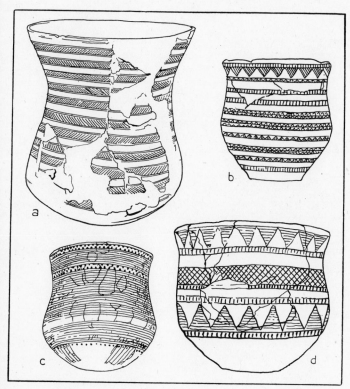

FIG. 36. Beakers from the Pyrenees and south-east France: *a.* Pagobakoitza Aizkorri, Guipuzcoa; *b.* and *d.* Saint Vellier, south of France; *c.* Pla de Boix, east Pyrenees.

associations so near their point of origin, if A. del Castillo Yurrita is right, seems to us to be fatal to his hypothesis.

In north-east Spain are several caves containing evidence

of beaker culture, which passed from the Meseta along the upper part of the Ebro valley towards the coast near the east end of the Pyrenees or *vice versa*. Here again the flint and stone work is poor, metal rare though not entirely absent, while the pottery is plentiful and of good quality. In the sub-Pyrenean region, both east and west, the beaker and megalith cultures overlap and to some extent combine. In this region the megaliths are not great corbelled tombs or elaborate dolmens, but relatively simple; even those who argue that the simple forms precede the complex are disposed to agree that in this region these monuments are relatively late. This concentration of culture at the east and west ends of the Pyrenees has led Leeds to believe that they represent a cultural movement coming from France into Spain, while others hold that it passed in the opposite direction. This latter view has doubtless been influenced by the idea that the beaker originated in Spain; we, who are advocating the hypothesis that it reached the Iberian peninsula from central Europe, are inclined to agree with Leeds, though neither he nor we desire to be dogmatic.

In southern France we find beaker pottery associated with megaliths of a simple type, which sometimes have yielded small objects of copper, chiefly beads; these occur throughout Languedoc, on the fringes of the Rhône valley right up to Haute Savoie. There is one corbelled tomb at Collorgues in the department of Gard. This culture in the south of France is, it is agreed, closely related to that found immediately south of the Pyrenees. There are hundreds of dolmens in the departments of Aveyron, Ardèche, Lot, Gard, Lozère, and Hérault, though some of these may be of a slightly later date.

There are, however, in southern France other contemporary monuments of a somewhat different type. Such are the megalithic tombs near Arles, of which the Grotto des Fées is the best known example. Hemp has recently shown that

these were the work of men who were familiar with the idea
of the gallery-dolmen, but who were excavating their tombs
in rocks with horizontal stratification instead of building them
up with great stones. These monuments are thus structurally
related to some of those in the Balearic Islands. They have
yielded a quantity of callais beads, said to number 113; this
may be taken as evidence of cultural links with the Atlantic sea-
board of France, either over land or by sea around the coasts of
the Iberian peninsula. Few callais beads have been found in the

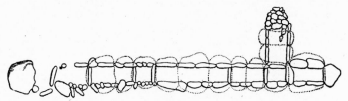

FIG. 37. Plan of the gallery-dolmen of La Halliade.

simple dolmens, but these have yielded a small number of amber
beads, thus emphasizing the distinctness of amber and callais.

Gallery-dolmens, this time not excavated in the rock but
built of great stones, occur also at and near La Halliade in
south-west France, just north of the Pyrenees. These are
closely related to those found in west Portugal and Brittany,
and, appropriately enough, have yielded callais beads; they
have also yielded beaker pottery, some of which in its decoration resembles that found in Brittany, Britain, and north-west
Europe. There can be no doubt that there is some link between
La Halliade and one, at least, of the cultural elements that
distinguish Brittany from Portugal, but it is interesting to note
that the three great Breton monuments, which have yielded rich
stores of callais, contained no beakers.

The megalithic and beaker cultures of Sardinia and the
Balearic Islands are generally believed to be extensions of those

of Spain; their corridor rock-cut tombs are found again near Arles, while beakers have been found in Sicily, where rock-cut tombs are the rule.

Traces of beaker culture have been found in caves near Lucca; and on the mainland of Italy at Remedello in the north, beakers, bracers, and fine flint work have been met with. These beakers admittedly resemble most closely some found in a cist in the French Maritime Alps. The megalithic tombs that occur near Taranto, in the south-east of Italy, are of fairly simple type and are generally considered to be of later date. No other megalithic tombs have been found in the peninsula.

Summing up, we see that an intrusive megalithic culture developed to a high level during the copper age in the southern half of the Iberian peninsula. Here, according to many writers, originated the beaker culture, which we believe to have been brought in from central Europe. It is our view that the two cultures met and mingled in the south of the peninsula, as well as in the region just south of the Pyrenees, southern France, Sardinia, and the Balearic Islands. The beaker culture reached north Italy, but here the idea of megalithic tombs was not introduced.

It is uncertain whether or not these north Italian sites lay on the trade route between Spain and central Europe, though it should be remembered that the province of Brescia, in which many of them occur, is clearly related to Alpine passes. If the route did not traverse north Italy, it may have passed through Haute Savoie, which has beakers and megaliths.

We cannot help thinking that the beaker and megalith cultures are quite distinct in origin, and first come into contact with one another in the megalithic areas of Denmark, Holland, Britain, and the Iberian peninsula. Had the beaker culture arisen in south Spain, it appears to us that with its spread to central Europe it would have carried the custom of erecting megalithic tombs, unless, which seems improbable, the inland people, being dwellers on the forest margin, constructed similar tombs in timber, of which we have no evidence.

BOOKS

FERGUSSON, JAMES. *Rude Stone Monuments* (London, 1872).
KENDRICK, T. D. *The Axe Age* (London, 1925).
PEET, T. ERIC. *Rough Stone Monuments and their Builders* (London, 1912).

7

Brittany and Northern France

IN Brittany the southern departments of Le Morbihan and Finistère are very rich in megalithic monuments; but, whereas those in Le Morbihan include magnificent gallery-dolmens, closely akin to those of Portugal, the tombs of Finistère are different. Several monuments of Le Morbihan, three in particular, have yielded a large collection of callais beads, as have those in Portugal; in Finistère callais is absent but amber is found. Fine axes of jadeite and other choice stones have been found in Le Morbihan but not in the other department. Lastly, beaker pottery is known from forty-two sites in Le Morbihan, whereas it occurs on only six sites in Finistère.

This suggests close connexion between Le Morbihan and the west of the Iberian peninsula, and much of the Breton beaker pottery is like the wares of Portugal and Spanish Galicia. In the copper age, or at its dawn, there began a maritime connexion between the west of the Iberian peninsula and Brittany. As knowledge accumulates, more and more does this link stand out; we have evidence of it in the later periods of the Bronze Age, in the La Tène phase of the Iron Age, in post-Roman times, and it is attested by the pilgrimages to Santiago da Compostella during the Middle Ages.

Whatever view one holds as to the place of origin of beakers,

there can be little doubt that the great majority of those found
in Brittany came by sea from the south. A few, however, from
Conguel, Er Roch, Mané Lud, and Kerallant in Le Morbihan and
from Rosmeur in Finistère, like one vessel from La Halliade in
the south of France, seem to be related to the cord-ornamented
beakers of Britain and to some from central Europe.   Some
beakers from Finistère also have the higher thinner form that is
usual in Britain rather than the broad bell form known in Spain.

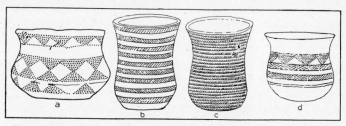

Fig. 38. Breton beakers from Loire Inférieure, Le Morbihan, and Finistère:
a. St. Nazaire, Loire Inférieure; *b*. Penmarc'h, Finistère; *c*. Plovan, Finistère;
d. Carnac, Le Morbihan.

Brittany has yielded a number of perforated battle-axes of
stone, for the most part of a rather early type, since the hole
is not in the middle but approaches one end, which is rounded.
This type of battle-axe was at this period characteristic of the
culture of northern Europe, and spread into Britain, to a less
extent into France, but did not reach the Iberian peninsula.
In the last-named area we find heavy stone axes with a groove
from the attachment of a thong. Axes of this type occur
occasionally in Britain, where they have been found in Wales
and at Alderley Edge in Cheshire; the Alderley Edge examples
are thought by some authorities to date from a much later
time. It is not very likely that either of these forms was invented
on more than one occasion, though some believe that the
grooved stone battle-axes of America have an independent

origin. It seems probable that in the perforated battle-axes we may discern culture links between Brittany and Britain or north Europe, while the grooved axe-heads denote the connexion between that province and the Iberian peninsula.

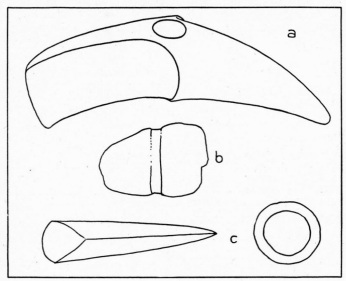

Fig. 39. *a*. Perforated battle-axe from Guernsey; *b*. Grooved battle-axe from the Iberian peninsula; *c*. Polished axe and ring of jadeite from Mané-er-Hroèk, Le Morbihan.

The typical flint arrow-heads of Portugal have barbs but no tangs. Careful search in the Breton collections has revealed few of these; nearly all the arrow-heads from this province have a tang as well as barbs. In this, Brittany resembles Britain and most parts of central and southern France. In Ireland, however, about 15 or 20 per cent. of the barbed arrow-heads are stemless, while more than 90 per cent. are of this type in Denmark and the west Baltic region. In this matter, then,

Brittany resembles France and Britain rather than the Iberian peninsula, which, curiously enough, resembles Ireland and the west Baltic region.

These are positive indications, but a negative one is no less striking. The splendid flint work found in the Iberian peninsula, Ireland, and the west Baltic region represents efforts to copy in flint fine daggers and curved blades of weapons seen in metal. This type of work is lacking in Brittany, where, on the other hand, the art of grinding and polishing stone was widespread, as it appears to have been also in Britain and in the Iberian peninsula. That Britain, with its ample supply of flint, lacks the splendid daggers of this material just mentioned should warn us against assuming that their absence in Brittany was due to the scarcity of flint there, and to the fact that the honey-coloured flint of Le Grand Pressigny, imported at that time, did not lend itself to the manufacture of such implements, since it chipped into long and sharp-edged flakes.

The absence of fine flint daggers from Brittany indicates that we are not dealing simply with a direct transplantation of culture from Portugal. None the less the use of choice materials like jadeite, nephromelanite, and chloromelanite, for stone axes and rings, is a link between these two regions. Crawford has described some axes of these fine materials, found in the south of England, and has pointed out that these indicate connexions with Brittany; otherwise they are rare in Britain and there appears to be no record of their discovery in the west Baltic region. Some of these choice materials have actually been found in the rocks of Le Morbihan.

On the whole, therefore, the objects belonging to the mega-lithic period found in Brittany show that this region had con-nexions, on the one hand with La Halliade and with Portugal, and on the other with Britain and north-west Europe. Amber beads, a northern link, are known from the department of

Finistère, but none from Le Morbihan until fairly late in the Bronze Age. Statements to the contrary have been made and have been copied from book to book, but these are incorrect. On the other hand callais, so abundant in Le Morbihan and in Portugal, is entirely lacking in the British Isles.

In the south of France occurs a variant of the representations of the human figure on schist palettes, in which a conventional- ized human figure is graven, not on a stone plaque but on a

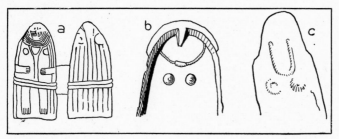

FIG. 40. Conventionalized figures from: *a.* Aveyron; *b.* the Marne; *c.* Guernsey.

fairly large standing stone; this idea is found also in the Marne area, but is absent from Brittany, though the idea of engraving designs on the walls, and sometimes on the roofs, of megalithic tombs is here carried to its highest pitch of development and has provided material for speculative interpretation of symbols. It is all the more strange, therefore, that in Guernsey, where the megalithic tombs closely resemble those in Le Morbihan, there are representations of the female figure, not only on a roofing-stone of a dolmen but on standing stones, though the latter are of unknown age and probably younger than the early megalithic and beaker cultures.

While a fair amount of copper has been found in Iberian megalithic tombs, it is very scarce in those of Brittany, and is completely absent from the corresponding monuments of

Britain and the west Baltic region. These last need not, therefore, belong to a pre-metal age, if the fundamental idea spread
from the Iberian peninsula, where copper is found in the
monuments, to more northerly lands where it is lacking.

The fine corbelled tomb on the Ile Longue in Le Morbihan
demonstrates kinship with south Iberian tombs. According to
Forde there is corbelling at Kerheuret in Finistère and at
Kerusan in Le Morbihan; in both these cases metal daggers
were found in the monuments. Corbelling on any extended
scale is very rare in the Breton monuments of this period. The
example at New Grange in Ireland must not conceal the broad
fact that this art is also rare in the British Isles, though partial
corbelling exists at La Hougue Bie, the largest monument of
Breton type in Jersey, in some long barrows in England, and,
as Hemp has shown, in one or two of the monuments in north
Wales. Partial corbelling, again, is found here and there in
the west Baltic region.

In the Breton gallery-dolmen the junction of the corridor
and chamber is sometimes marked by a projecting door-frame
and step. In most cases the dolmen is still, or was originally,
covered by a mound, though in some cases this may have
reached only to the top of the walls leaving the roof uncovered.

The typical gallery-dolmen of Le Morbihan, like that of the
Iberian peninsula, is one in which the chamber is an oval or
almost rectangular expansion of the corridor, the longest axis
of the former continuing the axis of the latter. Forde has,
however, described monuments in Finistère, in which the long
axis of a more or less rectangular chamber lies at right angles
to the line of the corridor. This form is rare in Britain, but is
typical in the west Baltic region and common in Holland.
This resemblance between the monuments of Finistère and
those in the north is in keeping with the discoveries of amber
in the former region.

Sometimes the chamber is not distinct from the corridor, and the whole monument is one long corridor, straight or crooked; this type is known as an *allée couverte*. As in the Iberian

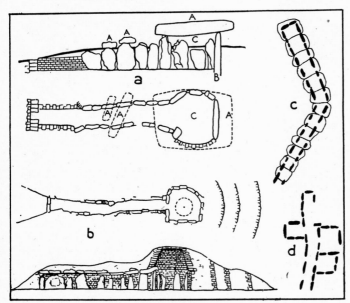

FIG. 41. Plans of Breton megalithic tombs of different types: *a.* Gallery-dolmen, Table des marchands, Locmariaquer; *b.* Corbelled tomb on Ile Longue; all in the department of Le Morbihan; *c.* Dolmen du Rocher, Plougoumelen; *d.* Klud-er-yer, Kériaval, Carnac.

peninsula, especially in its remoter parts, so in Brittany we find simple dolmens, many of them now, at any rate, not covered by a mound; many once had a corridor. We feel convinced, as do Le Rouzic and Forde, that both in Brittany and in the Iberian peninsula the corbelled tomb is the earlier type, and that the simple dolmen, with one or two capstones supported on a few uprights, more or less enclosing a chamber, is a derivative.

There are in Brittany a number of graves, like boxes of stone, known as cists; some have yielded bronze and all appear to be later than the dolmens. At Le Mont Saint Michel (Carnac), at Tumiac, in the peninsula of Rhuis on the south side of Le Morbihan Gulf, and at Mane'-er-Hroèk at Locmariaquer, on the opposite side of the entrance to the gulf, are immense mounds containing chambers, partly of dry walling, but not approached by corridors. These had been closed up, apparently, directly after the interments had taken place. These closed chambers have yielded splendid polished axes of jadeite and other choice stones and large collections of callais beads, but no beaker pottery. They may, therefore, represent a slightly different culture, perhaps contemporary with the gallery-dolmens.

Remarkable alignments as it were mark off the southern part of Le Morbihan between the estuary of La Trinité and that of Étel, or would do so were they restored to their original length. The direction of these long lines varies somewhat on both sides of a west to east orientation. In some cases the standing stones, in four or five rows, increase in size as they approach the west end, and at this end of the alignments at Menec, near Carnac, there are considerable remains of a fine semicircle of standing stones; these nearly touch one another, thus differing from the British stone circles. Le Rouzic has shown that one of the alignments passes over a Bronze Age monument, so we must attribute the alignments to that age or later. They represent a late development of Breton megalithic civilization, just as Stonehenge and Avebury may be considered special developments of a like culture in Britain.

Le Rouzic has studied the interesting stone circles at Er-Lannic, an island in the Gulf which gives the name of Morbihan to the department. Here the circles more nearly resemble those found in Britain. There are very few other examples in the province, but what appear to be the remains of another at

St. Germain near Étel are of special interest, for in this case a church and churchyard are within the circle. That this is not a mere chance is indicated by the fact that the same thing occurs at Yspytty Cynfyn, near Devil's Bridge in Cardiganshire, Wales, and there are traces of it elsewhere in that country. Here we seem to be dealing with a continuity of local consecra-

FIG. 42. Dolmen of Confolens.

tion from pagan to Christian times. We know on the one hand that the Celtic Church made much of that continuity; on the other hand we read that many Church Councils during the Dark Ages fulminated against the rites at great stone monuments, in spite of which some of these rites, sometimes in a Christianized garb, are still performed to-day. At Confolens in west France a dolmen has had the supporting stones replaced by round pillars with carved capitals of the eleventh or twelfth century.

It seems probable that in the early age of metal the land lay some metres higher above the sea than now, for the stone circles on the island of Er-Lannic now lie well below high-tide mark. If that was so, the Mor Braz, the sea outside the Gulf of Morbihan, but still separated from the Bay of Biscay by the remnants of the peninsula of Quiberon and the islands of Houat, Hoedic, and Belle Île, would have afforded a valuable and

FIG. 43. Entrance to a cist near Paris.

sheltered entry for coasting vessels, with an abundance of alternative landings to suit varied conditions of wind and tide. Finistère would have offered similar attractions for landing but would have lacked the shelter. Then there were valuable raw materials, such as jadeite, fibrolite, and various diorites, as well as other varieties of hard stone, suitable for manufacture of polished axes; moreover it has been suggested, though not proved, that callais may have been found here too. Again, it is probable that tin and gold were worked. Siret has gone so far as to suggest that the islands of the Mor Braz are the famous Cassiterides. On the other hand it is far from certain that the

tin and gold deposits were rich enough to attract the attention
of these early traders.

The peninsula of Brittany stands out into the Atlantic, and
the little vessels of the early traders from Portugal and Galicia
could coast along as far as Le Morbihan, but would need great
pluck to venture round the Pointe d'Audierne and the signifi-
cantly named Baie des Trépassés, or Bay of the Dead, still more
to sail near the rocky reefs of Ushant. There are many, though
poorer, evidences of megalithic culture along the north coast
of Brittany and the west of Normandy; it is no great distance
to the Channel Islands, rich in megaliths, and on the way to
England. The Breton peninsula was thus marked out by nature
to be a central place of call between the Iberian peninsula and
the south of France on the one side, and Ireland, Britain, and
north-west Europe on the other.

At Kerlescant there was once a dolmen with a specially made
entrance, formed by concavities combined to make a circular
hole; this type of hole has been termed a 'port-hole'. Now such
port-holes in passage graves occur in the department of Seine-
et-Oise; similar holes occur also in the Marne valley, though
here in tombs hollowed out of the rock instead of being built
up with great stones. In the Marne valley, too, has been found
one callais bead, an indication, small but clear, of some connexion with Brittany. The Marne region, however, shares the
idea of the rock-cut tomb, not with Brittany but with Provence
and the Balearic Islands. The Marne culture also shares with
that of the south of France the idea of the standing-stone
engraved to represent a conventionalized female figure. The
Marne area may therefore be said to have links both with
Brittany and with the south of France, and serves as a useful
reminder of the very general fact that a regional culture, in
almost every case known at this or any other period, has links
not only in one but in several different directions. The mixture

of diverse culture-elements has stimulated thought and initiative, has prevented the hardening of habit, and so has led men on to new efforts and to new flowerings of civilization.

BOOKS

KENDRICK, T. D *The Axe Age* (London, 1925). KENDRICK, T. D. *The Archaeology of the Channel Islands*, vol. i (London, 1928).

8

The West Baltic Region

IN our second volume, *Hunters and Artists*, we described the shell-mounds of the Baltic and the epipalaeolithic culture of which these remains are evidence. We pointed out, too, that during the second or Ertebölle phase of that culture, rough pottery came into use. This we discussed again in the first chapter of our third volume, *Peasants and Potters*. The presence of this pottery in the shell-mounds of the Baltic has led some writers to think that pottery evolved independently in this region. It is well, however, to remember that we cannot really date the Ertebölle culture, and that, though its beginnings may be much earlier than those of the metal age in Europe, we cannot be sure how late it lasted. In fact it is reasonable to suppose that it continued until replaced by the higher civilization that we are going to describe in this chapter; if so, for a time the two cultures must have existed side by side, and, in fact, near Stockholm a very similar culture persisted until a much later date. On the whole, therefore, we think it likely that the potter's art was introduced into this region by those who brought with them other new elements of culture, and that this art was acquired from them by the Ertebölle folk; certain resemblances, pointed out by Childe, between the shell-mound pottery and some from El Garcel in Spain, seem to indicate the direction from which this art arrived.

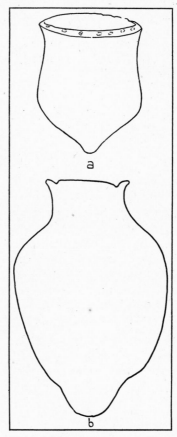

The megalithic culture of the west Baltic region reaches its highest development in Zealand, the largest of the Danish islands, especially in the neighbourhood of Ros-kilde Fjord. It is so rich that some have even suggested that the culture arose in this region, a view which, we think, can be dismissed at once in the light of what has been written in the earlier chapters of this volume. On the mainland of Jutland the megalithic monuments lie near the eastern shore and in the north; whereas most of the promontory was occu-pied, apparently at the time when they were erected, by a people with a different civi-lization, known as that of the single-graves. This civiliza-tion, too, has been claimed by some to have arisen here, and to have spread south-wards to the base of the

Fig. 44. Pots from: *a*. Viby, Denmark; *b*. El Garcel, Spain.

peninsula, where all trace of it is lost. The perforated stone battle-axe is such a prominent feature of this single-grave civili-

zation, that this weapon has in consequence been claimed to be
a Baltic invention. This, again, we cannot accept, and our view

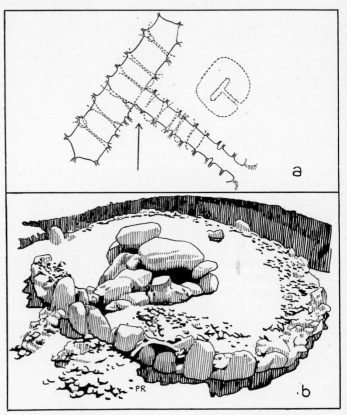

FIG. 45. West Baltic dolmens: *a.* Kong Askers Høj, Møen, Denmark;
b. Mejls, north of Varde, Denmark.

is now shared by the best Danish and by some Swedish writers.
Megaliths occur in enormous numbers in Denmark, along
the Swedish coast of the Cattegat, and in the province of Scanai

at the southern end of Sweden; they are found also in Vester-
gotland, Vermland, Örebro, and Södermanland, the central
zone of the Swedish lakes. There are also some in the island of
Öland in the Baltic, but these were thought by Montelius to
be relatively late. A number of these monuments somewhat
resemble the gallery-dolmens of Le Morbihan and Portugal,
and have the long axis of the chamber in line with the corridor;
such monuments are, however, relatively few in number.
There are a large number of simple dolmens, as there are in
most regions in Europe where megaliths occur, but the most
characteristic monument in this area is one in which the long
axis of the chamber is at right angles to the line of the corridor,
giving the structure the form of a T.

Some of the T-shaped monuments are partially corbelled.
A scheme of corbelling has been begun, and three or four rows
of stones have been laid, each row projecting farther in than
the one beneath it; but the corbelling has rarely been carried
beyond these few rows, and the main part of the roof consists
of enormous blocks of stone. The monuments are often covered
by high and conspicuous mounds, and around the bases of
many of these there are rings of standing stones. We do not
wish to over-emphasize the importance of the various shapes of
the monuments found in different regions, but it seems to be
worth while to note that T-shaped megaliths occur in Ireland
and the Breton department of Finistère, and that in both
regions amber has been found. The same type of monument
occurs also in north-west Germany and in the north of Holland;
we think, therefore, that these two last areas represent expansions of the west Baltic megalith region.

The distribution of the megalithic monuments of the west
Baltic region so near to the coast leaves us in no doubt that
this civilization arrived by sea, almost certainly from the
Iberian peninsula; it is possible that Ireland was a station on

the way, but it is difficult at present to offer any detailed suggestions as to the route or the points of entry. Roskilde Fjord is a remarkable inlet on the north coast of Zealand, wonderfully protected, for it opens into another fjord more or less parallel to it, and only through this does it communicate with the sea.

FIG. 46. Megalithic pottery from the west Baltic region: *a*. Tovstrup, Hind Herred; *b*. Fyen; *c*. Skarpsalling, Slet Herred; all in Denmark.

Here was a district with land suitable for agriculture and with great possibilities for fishing. We have already noted that both in Brittany and in the Iberian peninsula the old megalithic centres have retained their tradition of sanctity to this day, and that the cult of Santiago da Compostella, the most sacred spot in Spain, took its origin from a megalithic monument. It is interesting to note, too, that Roskilde Fjord is the centre of Danish tradition, and that Roskilde cathedral, in the fine old city at the head of the fjord, is the focus of Denmark's religious ceremonial.

The megalithic pottery of the west Baltic region differs from that of Brittany and from that of the chief megalithic centres of the Iberian peninsula, for it includes very little that can be considered as belonging to the beaker culture in the strict

sense of the term. In Brittany, and to some extent in the
Iberian peninsula as well, the pottery of the beaker type contrasts sharply with other pots found in the monuments, for it
has been more thoroughly baked and is usually of a finer paste.

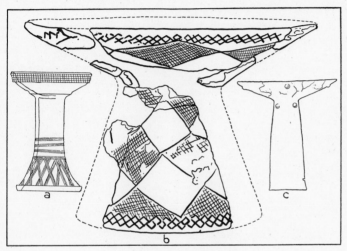

FIG. 47. Pots on stand from: *a*. Kish, Mesopotamia; *b*. Denmark;
c. Lengyel, Hungary.

This is not so in the west Baltic region, where the pots found
in the megaliths, though unlike the beakers and the wares
associated with them, are extraordinarily fine and well made.
They include splendid carinated pots, resembling and doubtless
related to those of Brittany and Portugal, but of much finer
make. In some cases the ornament seems to have been impressed
upon the pot by a cockle-shell, and one of the pots is probably
the finest prehistoric vessel known from any region or period.

A few of the west Baltic pots of this period, dating possibly
from towards its close, are decorated with a pair of eyes, and
sometimes with series of triangles set in horizontal rows; these

H 2

288372

features occur also in Brittany and the Iberian peninsula. The use of the triangle decoration may perhaps be due to influence received from the beaker culture, though this is by no means certain. A new feature in the west Baltic region is the use of long horizontal lugs, pierced for suspension.

There is one pot in particular that helps us to appreciate the fineness of the potter's art in the megalithic civilization of this region as compared with all the wares from other centres of this period, except those of the beaker culture. This famous vessel is a shallow dish on a high stand, which has the form of a truncated cone. Childe has described pots of this kind found at Lengyel in Hungary and elsewhere in central Europe, while shallow dishes on high stands of a more complicated form, in which the upper part of the truncated cone has become modified into a pillar, have been discovered in Cemetery A at Kish in Mesopotamia. The dishes on a high foot, found at El Argar in south-east Spain, and on other sites in the Mediterranean basin, seem to be different in design and can hardly be the prototypes of this west Baltic example, though they, too, may be ultimately derived from the Mesopotamian forms.

It would seem that it was such influences from the south-east, from Hungary and from beyond, that caused the megalithic civilization in the west Baltic region so to excel in its pottery; no such advanced influences reached Brittany from continental sources. In the Iberian peninsula the pottery of the megalithic civilization was vastly improved by contact with the beaker culture; this is equally true whatever view we take of the origin of the latter. Similar influences were felt in the west Baltic region, but before we discuss this we must describe other objects found in the megalithic tombs.

An outstanding Baltic feature is the excellence of its flint work. Both in the megaliths and elsewhere are found numbers of large flint axes with parallel sides and edges at right-angles to them. These are characteristic of this region and usually exhibit a combination of chipping and grinding. They contrast sharply with the polished pointed-butted axes, made of crystalline stones, found in the Breton megaliths. A large number of

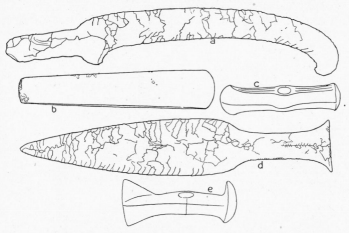

FIG. 48. Fine flint-work from Denmark: *a*. Dagger from Favrskov, Baag Herred; *b*. Axe from Jegstrup, Nørlyng Herred. Stone battle-axes from: *c*. Daugstrup, Lunde Herred, and *e*. Aagesholm, Smørum Herred; *d*. Dagger from Borre, Møen.

heavy flint chisels of the same type have also been found in Denmark and elsewhere in the west Baltic region.

Flint arrow-heads are another conspicuous feature; over 90 per cent. of these, as we have already mentioned, have concave bases and no stems. None of the arrow-heads of this region are quite so elaborate as the finest specimens from Egypt, North Africa, and the Iberian peninsula, but the average specimen is nevertheless very well made. All these implements are, however, excelled by the splendid flint daggers, knives, and sickle-like blades to which reference has already been made in chapter 6. They are, if possible, finer than those from the

Iberian peninsula, and there can be no shadow of doubt that a great many of them are imitations in flint of originals that had been made in metal.

The megalithic tombs of the west Baltic region are usually described as belonging to the Stone Age; this statement, however, should, we believe, be accepted with reserve. It seems highly probable that metal did not reach the prehistoric people of the west Baltic region either very early or in great quantity, but the forms of the flint daggers found there suggest that these folk were not entirely ignorant of copper. The earliest metal implements found in the tombs in this region are of very advanced types. These belong to the Bronze Age, and not even to the earliest phase of that, and include swords as well as highly evolved forms of bronze axes. The use of metal, and the knowledge of alloying it, had therefore, had a long history before the first metal object was laid in a Baltic tomb. That metal had been known for some part, at any rate, of this time in or near the Baltic region is clear from the fact that a fair number of early bronze and some copper axes have been found there, though not in tombs. This suggests that metal was for long rare in this district, and the need for the economical use of this precious material, or religious conservatism, led to the continued use of stone for grave goods after metal implements had come into general use. Both Stjerna and Brögger believe that copper, at any rate, had been introduced into Scandinavia by the time that the gallery-dolmens were being built.

Before describing in further detail the contents of the megalithic tombs, we must say something of the single-grave civilization of this region; this is best developed in Jutland, but is found also in Zealand and in the neighbouring parts of Sweden. Graves of this type are very numerous, and in a number of cases a body has been buried over an earlier grave, so that we have some indications of a chronological sequence. The earliest graves contain pottery, some of it of the beaker type; these are of the bulb-and-neck variety, decorated with cord impressions, but none of the bell-beaker form. Far more characteristic, how-

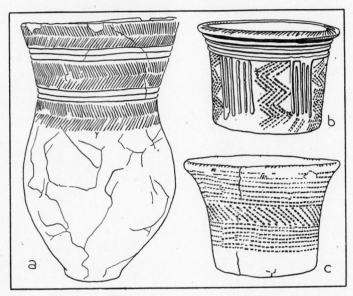

FIG. 49. *a.* Beaker from single-grave at Slauggaard, Slaugs Herred; and Pots, derived from beakers, from single-graves at: *b.* Askjaergaarde, Nørvang Herred; and *c.* Brande, Nørvang Herred.

ever, of this civilization than the strictly beaker pottery are pots of simpler, almost cylindrical form, derived from beaker types. These have been found in great numbers and seem to indicate that the single-grave civilization had received strong influences from that of the beaker-people of north central Europe. This view is supported by the presence in many of the single graves of 'bracers', so often found in association with beakers elsewhere.

An interesting feature is that some single graves and a few megalithic tombs show intermingling of the two cultures, battle-axes occurring in the megaliths and megalithic pottery

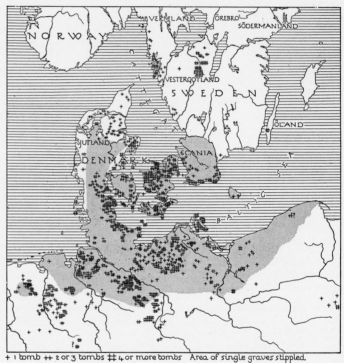

FIG. 50. Map of the west Baltic region.

in the single graves. We agree with Müller and Kjaer that ultimately the two civilizations fused, and the cist, a simplification of the dolmen, became the typical tomb, being used for a single individual instead of for a family or community. The same feature is noticeable elsewhere, and it would appear that the practice of erecting an ossuary was abandoned as time went on in most of the megalithic centres.

Considering the marked distinctness of the megalithic civilization in the west Baltic region from the cultures of central Europe, we feel justified in believing that its interests were mainly maritime; we think that it had relations, by way of Ireland, with the Iberian peninsula, a sea-route presenting many difficulties and one that cannot have been used except in favourable weather. Thus the development of megalithic civilization in the Baltic must have been to some extent independent of its growth elsewhere, and, as we have seen, it received several contributions from central Europe. The single-grave civilization, on the other hand, seems to have been essentially continental, spreading northwards towards the megalith area from the north European plain. The ultimate intermingling of the two, and the beginning of commerce with Bohemia, marks the rise of the splendid Bronze Age civilization of the Baltic, which we shall describe in a later volume. We believe that the megalith and single-grave period in the west Baltic region lasted for at least several centuries. This helps to explain the enormous number of tombs and casual 'finds', and the remarkable variety displayed in the objects, especially in the pottery, notwithstanding that certain standard types persisted throughout.

In some of the more remote parts of Sweden dolmens are found with 'port-holes'. These occur also in Germany, and something analogous has been found in two of the English long barrows, and at Plas Newydd in Anglesey, while one was claimed by Montelius in the Isle of Man. There is a holed dolmen in Belgium, and the idea occurs in the monuments of Seine-et-Oise and in Jersey. The dolmens or stone cists of the Caucasus, Syria, Palestine, and India, usually have such holes, and it has been suggested that the idea reached the Baltic from the south-east.

It may have done so, since there seems reason for believing that the perforated battle-axe reached Denmark from that quarter.

We prefer, however, to leave the matter without expressing too definite an opinion at present, merely urging that the study of west Baltic civilization reveals most strikingly the fact that European life, even in the remote times that we have been describing, was already being knit into a network of cultural expansions and interchanges. Life here was showing a vigour unknown before, and this we ascribe to the development of settled life with agriculture and to the growth of maritime commerce. The one gave an assured food supply, the other secured the inhabitants from falling under the domination of habit with the consequent cramping of initiative. None the less it is well to note that nowhere in west Europe, save perhaps in south-east Spain, have we evidence of the existence at this time of anything worthy of the name of a city, though cities had long been important features in western Asia, Egypt, and the Aegean region.

BOOKS

CHILDE, V. GORDON. *The Dawn of European Civilization* (London, 1925).
KENDRICK, T. D. *The Axe Age* (London, 1925).

9

The British Isles

UNTIL recently it was universally believed that the axe of ground or polished stone, the type object of the Neolithic Age, was of immense antiquity in north-west Europe, and that it had been derived, either in one region or in several, from some tool of palaeolithic or epipalaeolithic form. While we cannot deny that in its shape it may have an epipalaeolithic ancestry, it is becoming increasingly clear that the art of grinding and polishing these tools was introduced from the south-east, together with the potter's art, agriculture, and domestic animals, and that all these arts were derived from a civilization familiar with gold and copper. That the knowledge of pottery, grain, and domestic animals, together with the art of grinding

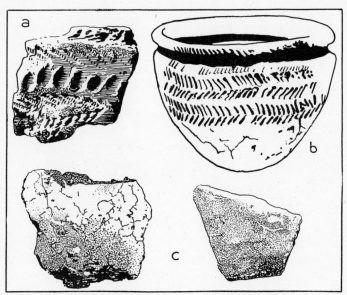

FIG. 51. Fragments of neolithic pottery from: *a.* West Kennet; *b.* the Mortlake bowl; *c.* Wexcombe.

stone, spread farther and faster than metallurgy is not surprising when we remember that metal ores are scarce, that the working of metals is a highly specialized art, and that, until the discovery of bronze, metal objects were rather articles of luxury than implements of everyday use. For this reason we are now looking upon neolithic civilization as the herald of metal, and not as an independent culture evolved in western Europe from that of epipalaeolithic times.

The study of 'neolithic' sites has revealed beaker pottery, sometimes associated with what is considered true neolithic ware, and also two other types that Menghin has termed *Grimston-Keramik* and *Peterborough-Keramik*. The former has a dark and imperfectly fired paste, showing a large amount of white grit and crushed shell. It has been found in a number of long barrows in Gloucestershire and Wiltshire, beneath a long barrow at Wexcombe in the latter county and at Hanging Grimston in Yorkshire. The latter, heavily decorated with impressions of twisted thongs, finger-tip impressions, and ridges, and ragged finger-nail scratches, is best known from the long barrow at West Kennet, from Peterborough, and from Mortlake. One might, perhaps, better call the first Wexcombe and the second West Kennet ware.

Mr. and Mrs. Alexander Keiller have found at Windmill Hill, near Avebury, an early settlement, defended by three concentric ditches, placed at a considerable distance apart, and within some of these were rows of holes that had held posts. The ditches are of varying depth, the deepest point being 9 ft. 6 in., but they are intermittent, leaving at intervals wide unexcavated entrances, that remind us of Urmitz and other villages of the Michelsberg culture described in an earlier chapter. This feature had already in 1911 been noticed by Mrs. Cunnington in the earlier settlement at Knap Hill, overlooking the Vale of Pewsey, and what appears to be a similar structure has lately been reported from the Sussex downs.

In the two outer ditches at Windmill Hill the excavators distinguished three layers, of which the middle one contained nothing but a few small fragments, similar to those in the top layer, from which they had apparently worked their way down. This indicates two periods of occupation, divided by a period in which the settlement had been abandoned. In the top layer were found innumerable fragments of beakers and of both the other wares, the West Kennet and the Wexcombe, as well as a number of other wares not yet described. These appear all to have been contemporary, and, since beakers have been found on several occasions with bronze implements of early type, we must assume that the later occupation of the Windmill Hill settlement took place not long before the introduction of

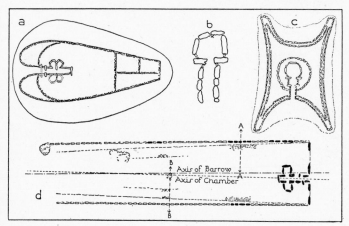

FIG. 52. Plans of British long barrows: *a*. Uley, Gloucestershire; *b*. West Kennet, Wiltshire; *c*. Horned cairn of Get, Caithness; *d*. Wayland's Smithy, Berkshire.

bronze into this country, and may have continued after that important event had occurred, though so far no metal object has been recovered from the site.

The wares from the bottom layer were not all the same, but they were all of them gritty, and in this resemble the *Grimston-Keramik* or Wexcombe ware, though they are much rougher fabrics. At the bottom was one type of a yellowish-brown colour, which seems to have been the earliest to be made at this site. Reconstructions by Mrs. Keiller show either rough ovoid pots or hemispherical bowls with horizontal lugs and bear a fairly close resemblance to the *westische Keramik* of Switzerland and to some of the pots found on Michelsberg sites, though the characteristic tulip-shaped vase has not yet come to light on this site. At the very bottom of the outer ditch were found saddle querns, evidence of the cultivation of grain.

If we are right in deriving the Michelsberg culture from that of the *westische Keramik*, and in believing that the latter reached Switzerland from the Rhône-Saône region, it seems probable that it was from the latter region that the knowledge of agriculture and the potter's art spread to the north of France and to Britain, though farther excavations in eastern France are needed before the question can be settled.

After an interval, probably of short duration, another influence reached this island. This was the civilization of the long barrows and with it, it would appear, the West Kennet ware or *Peterborough-Keramik*. Long barrows are long mounds, with parallel sides on each of which there is a ditch; this ditch does not continue round the ends, one of which usually rises higher than the rest of the mound. They usually contain a megalithic chamber, sometimes a series of such chambers opening from a central gallery, though in a few cases no signs of such a chamber have been found. They occur most frequently in the Cotswolds and in Wiltshire, though there are a number in south-east Wales, as well as in Hampshire, Berkshire, and elsewhere. Two in Kent, Kit's Coty House on the Medway, and Coldrum some miles to the west, seem more closely to resemble the megalithic tombs found in the north of Holland. The others form a series by themselves, and do not closely resemble the tombs of the west Baltic region. Most of them have yielded fragments of West Kennet ware and in some cases fragments of beakers, but so far no metal objects have been found within them, so that they are believed to belong to the Neolithic Age. Reginald Smith, in discussing the Mortlake bowl and similar pottery from Peterborough, which belong to the West Kennet ware, showed that similar vessels occur in Finland and the east of Sweden. It is possible, therefore, that this may have come direct from the east Baltic. This area received most of its culture from Denmark, though it may have obtained other elements, notably hemispherical bowls like that found at Mortlake, through Fatjanovo from the Russian steppe.

The mixed cultural elements at Windmill Hill in its second period are indicated by Wexcombe ware, we think of Rhône-Saône origin, and West Kennet ware, of east Baltic origin, brought in by long-barrow people who had cultural links with the west Baltic region, Brittany, and Portugal, and the Russian steppe. Lastly, we have the beaker-folk, coming perhaps a little later, and reaching this country from the mouth of the Rhine.

The early people of the second period at Windmill Hill were long-headed and of slender build; so were the long-barrow folk. The beaker-folk, however, were of quite a different type. Their leaders, at any rate, seem to have been men rather above the average height, of strong build, with moderately broad heads; they had powerful faces with prominent brow ridges divided by a marked furrow. Their type, whether transmitted from this time or introduced with later invasions, is handed down in some well-known British families to this day, and is characteristic of certain regions in this country. In Scottish burials of this time, especially in Aberdeenshire, a broader-headed element of more characteristic Alpine type has been found in short cists, associated with beakers. Remains of this people with their characteristic pottery and other objects, such as bracers and perforated axe-hammers of stone, have been found in low circular burial mounds known as Round Barrows. These occur in most of the eastern counties of Great Britain from the Moray Firth to the Channel, and in the southern counties of England as far west as Dorset. Inland from these coastal entries the beaker culture spread fairly widely on the English plain, south-east of a line drawn from Lyme Regis to the Vale of Pickering, the area that remained of outstanding importance so long as Britain depended mainly on home-grown grain.

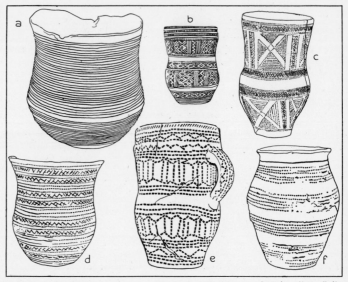

FIG. 53. British beakers from: *a*. Bathgate, Linlithgow; *b*. Eriswell, Suffolk; *c*. East Kennet, Wiltshire; *d*. Stogursey, Somerset; *e*. Cwm Du, Brecknock; *f*. Felixstowe, Suffolk.

Their barrows are specially numerous on Salisbury plain and in the Peak district, while remains of their civilization are not uncommon round Oxford.

Beakers have not been found in any numbers in the basins of the Dee and Severn; this seems to be due to the extensive marshes and forests that formerly existed in those regions. Farther west a few have been found in Devonshire, in south-east Wales, and in north Wales, while one with a handle has been discovered in Cornwall. In spite of these occurrences it is clear that the western promontories of Britain lay outside the beaker territory.

British beakers have for the most part smaller diameters in

FIG. 54. Bowls from: *a*. Algodor, Toledo, Spain; *b*. Down, Ireland; *c*. Ffostill, Brecknock.

proportion to their height than have the true bell-beakers of central Europe, Brittany, and the Iberian peninsula, but one from Linlithgow and a few from Wiltshire have a fairly typical bell form. Cord impression is common in their decoration, but incised lines, and lines formed by a series of points, are also found, and they are evidently closely related to the beakers of Holland and the Rhine basin. Associated with beakers have been found flint arrow-heads, especially those with barbs and stems almost equal in size reaching to a common base line, perforated stone axe-hammers, buttons with V-shaped perforations, bracers or bowmen's wrist guards consisting of rectangular stone plaques with two or three perforations at each end, axes and daggers of metal, which in most cases seems to be bronze rather than copper.

It was formerly believed that the people whose remains are found buried with beakers brought the knowledge of bronze into this country, and they were called the Bronze Age invaders of Britain. This view is held by some, while others believe that they acquired this knowledge after their arrival in this island. It is clear that when they arrived metal was well known in many parts of Europe, and they can hardly have been totally ignorant of its existence and use, but whether they actually possessed implements of this material and knew how to cast them is uncertain; if they possessed such objects, they were probably few in number and almost certainly of copper.

The slightness of direct 'beaker' influence on Ireland is notorious, but fragments of two beakers have been found near Moytura in County Sligo, and one, at least, of these fragments suggests the bell-beaker form and may be related rather to the beakers of Brittany and the Iberian peninsula than to those of Great Britain. That they were derived directly from the west of Europe is supported by the occurrence of two shallow vessels with rounded bases, on which are incised cross decorations like those found in the west of the Iberian peninsula. When we remember, too, that the very abundant flint arrow-heads of Ireland include a fair proportion with concave bases, that is to say with barbs and no stems, like those found in the west Baltic and the Iberian peninsula, we realize the probability that Ireland's contacts belonged to a coast-wise maritime movement rather than to a continental spread from central Europe.

Stemless flint arrow-heads are very uncommon in Great Britain and Brittany, while fine flint daggers are features of the Iberian peninsula, Ireland, and the west Baltic region. We seem, therefore, to have two independent but approximately contemporary movements. One of these passed from central Europe, down the Rhine, and reached the eastern shores of

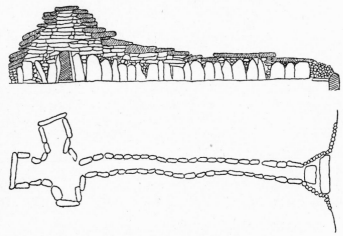

FIG. 55. New Grange in Ireland.

Great Britain; the other came by sea from Portugal, touching Le Morbihan, and arrived in Ireland, and passed thence by the west coast of Scotland around Caithness to Denmark and south Sweden, whence it spread to north Germany and Holland. That the latter of these movements touched the coast of Wales seems indicated by the discovery there of a shallow vessel with a rounded base; this was found by Vulliamy at Ffostill on the Welsh border and came from a monument that seems to be transitional between a long barrow and a cist.

The megalith culture of Ireland and the western part of

Great Britain seems to have been roughly contemporary with the beaker culture, as was the case in Holland. Its beginnings, however, especially in Ireland, may be placed somewhat earlier, as they may probably also in Denmark and more certainly, we believe, in Brittany and the Iberian peninsula. One of the most noteworthy features of this megalith culture is that its distribution, in the main, is complementary to that of the beaker culture. The Penwith peninsula of west Cornwall, Pembrokeshire, north-west Wales, and Anglesey, are important regions for megaliths, often of types simpler than those of Brittany and the Iberian peninsula, but showing attempts at corbelling as, for example, at Capel Garmon in North Wales. The long barrows also show similar efforts here and there. The megalith cultures of the western promontories of the west of England and Wales are, however, very inferior to those of Ireland, where the finest example is the corbelled tomb at New Grange, though there are other very notable monuments, such as that at Annaclochmullin, which recalls the 'Giants' graves in Sardinia, as does also one at Cashtal-yn-Ard, near Maughold, in the Isle of Man. There are a vast number of dolmens in Ireland and their kinship with those in Iberia, Brittany, and the west Baltic region is very apparent.

Although the long barrows of England and south-east Wales differ in plan, the construction of their chambers shows that they are ultimately derived from the megalithic tombs of the areas that we have been describing, though it is possible that they have been influenced by the stone cists found in the Crimea and the Caucasus. In Wiltshire long barrows have been opened but found to contain no chambers. Greenwell was of the opinion that this was due to the lack of suitable stone; it is possible, however, that they may originally have contained a wooden cist or chamber, such as was found at Maikop to the north of the Caucasus. Some monuments in east Yorkshire,

sometimes called long barrows, seem rather to have been two
or more round barrows joined together.

A series of cairns have been opened in the Isle of Arran by
Bryce; some have thought that these are related to the English
long barrows. This is suggested by their shape, but the internal
arrangements are different, for they contain a series of adjoining

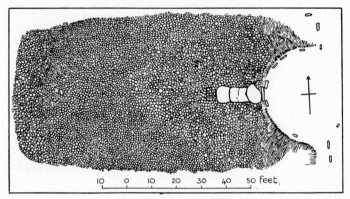

FIG. 56. Plan of Carn Ban, Kilmorey Water, Arran.

chambers but no passage. Great cairns of megalithic type occur
in the west of Scotland and are particularly abundant in Caithness; similar tombs occur also in the Orkneys. Though their
dates are uncertain, and some may have been erected long after
the period we are describing, it seems probable that they are
derived from those of Ireland and indicate points on the route
from that island to the west Baltic region.

Stone circles are probably somewhat younger than other
megaliths and have a different distribution. For instance, in
Scotland, as Bryce has shown, the megalithic tombs or cairns
are distributed along the west coast and over Caithness as far
as the Moray Firth, while the stone circles cover the eastern
plain from that point almost down to the English border.

Again, in Pembrokeshire, there are a number of dolmens on the northern slope, but none on the southern slope, of the Preseli (Prescelly) Hills, while about a dozen stone circles range from the summit to the plain on the south.

This easterly distribution of circles in Scotland, and a similar distribution in the north of England, suggests that this element reached Britain from the east or south-east. Rings of standing stones are found around some of the chambered barrows of

Fig. 57. Circle at Stennis, Orkney.

Denmark and the west Baltic region, and it is a reasonable suggestion that the British stone circles are derived from these. On the other hand a round barrow has been found in Holland, containing a beaker burial, which had been surrounded by a ring of vertically-set posts of wood, and, since traces of a similar circle of wooden posts have been found on Salisbury Plain by Mrs. Cunnington and named Woodhenge, it is possible that the custom of erecting circles was introduced into this country by the beaker-folk, and translated into stone when they came into contact with the megalith culture.

Whatever their origin, stone circles became more highly developed here than elsewhere, and there are in the British Isles a number of such monuments, of which the best known is Stonehenge. It is a reconstruction, with larger stones, of an earlier circle, the stones of which, re-dressed and somewhat reduced in size, were placed within the larger circle. These older stones, unlike the others which are sarsen stone or grey wethers, such as are found in great numbers on Salisbury Plain, are of non-local origin, and it has recently been shown that they must have been brought from the Preseli Hills in Pembrokeshire. This fact militates against the view that such circles were of beaker origin.

Larger and more complicated in structure is the great stone circle at Avebury, containing as it did two smaller circles within its ring, the whole surrounded by a deep ditch and high embankment; this was erected within a few miles of Windmill Hill. Hardly less in importance are the circles at Callernish in the island of Lewis and at Stennis in Orkney, while among lesser examples are Arbor Low and the Rollright stones.

We have endeavoured to show that men bearing the beaker culture spread westward from central Europe into Britain, where they shared the country with the people of the megalith culture, each people for the most part keeping to its special district. In this we have something analogous to what happened in Brittany, Holland, and the west Baltic region. In all these regions the two cultures overlapped to some extent, and in Wiltshire we have ample evidence of some such admixture. Under such conditions we should expect to find new and original types developing from the mingling of cultures, and it is not surprising to find the evolution of stone circles in Britain, with conspicuous examples in Wiltshire, and the great alinements in Brittany, most noticeable at Carnac in Le Morbihan.

BOOKS

ABERCROMBY, THE HON. JOHN. *A Study of the Bronze Age Pottery of Great Britain and Ireland* (Oxford, 1912).

CUNNINGTON, M. E. *The Pottery from the Long Barrow at West Kennet, Wilts.* (Devizes, 1927).

KENDRICK, T. D. *The Axe Age; a Study in British Prehistory* (London, 1925).

HOLMES, T. RICE. *Ancient Britain and the Invasion of Julius Caesar* (Oxford, 1907).

10

The First Dynasty of Babylon

IN *The Steppe and the Sown* we pointed out that, from the time of Sargon of Agade, the wild tribes on the borders had been threatening the prosperity of the cities of Mesopotamia, and that at length, in 2169 B.C., the Amurru had broken through their defences and had established themselves at Babylon, where Sumu-abu became the first king of the First Dynasty of that city.

The sudden rise to importance of Babylon, which had hitherto been a city of little note except as a religious centre, seems to have been due to one of those changes in the course of the Euphrates which have been not uncommon in its history. This change, while bringing Babylon to the front, led to the decay of Kish, which had hitherto stood upon its banks, and had up to now been one of the leading cities of Mesopotamia since the earliest days of legendary history. Sumu-abu was not able to make himself master of many of the cities of the plain, though he seems to have made his influence felt at Kish and in a few other towns close by. He appears to have rested content with this, and on his death in 2155 B.C. he was succeeded by Sumu-la-ilu, who in turn did not feel disposed to augment his territories. Soon after his accession he seems to have been afraid that the Sumerian cities of the south would deprive him even of Babylon, for in 2150 B.C. he fortified that city by erecting a great wall on the southern side. Relieved from fear in this direction he attacked Kish in 2143 B.C., and reduced it to a state of complete dependence. After this he was engaged only in peaceful occupations until his death in 2119 B.C., when he was succeeded by his son Zabum, who carried on the peaceful policy of his father.

Zabum was succeeded in 2105 B.C. by his son Abil-Sin or

Apil-Sin, who was no more aggressive than his predecessors, and he again in 2087 B.C. by his son Sin-muballit, who reigned peacefully until 2067 B.C., when he was followed by his son Hammurabi, who soon started on a series of conquests.

In the meantime the cities of Mesopotamia owed allegiance to one of the two predominant cities, Isin and Larsa, and the

FIG. 58. Figure of a dog of Sumu-ilu, from Telloh.

whole century that elapsed between the conquest of Sumu-abu and the death of Sin-muballit was taken up by a constant struggle for supremacy between these two states, varied occasionally by intervention on the part of the kings of Elam.

Bur-sin or Pur-sin, who was king of Isin at the time of the capture of Babylon, seems not to have been an energetic monarch, and the chief power was in the hands of Sumu-ilu, king of Larsa, who was steadily enlarging his dominions. In 2166 B.C. he attacked Kish, but was not able to annex that city to his kingdom, and after that he seems to have been content with the dominions that he had obtained, for we hear of no fresh wars before his death in 2141 B.C., when he was succeeded by Mur-Adad, who seems to have been of a peaceful disposition. He died in 2125 B.C., when he was succeeded by his son Sin-idinnam.

We must now return to Isin. In 2158 B.C. Bur-sin had been succeeded by his son Iter-pi-sin and he in turn in 2153 B.C. by his brother Girra-imti or Irra-imitti. He is said to have abdicated in favour of a gardener, Enlil-ibni, who was succeeded the following year by Enlil-bani, who seems to have been his son. It was his successor Zembya or Zambia (2121–2118 B.C.) who called in the aid of the king of Elam to help him to withstand the attacks of Sin-idinnam, king of Larsa.

Sin-idinnam called himself the benefactor of Ur, and claimed to be king of Larsa, Sumer, and Akkad. He seems to have been bent on bringing all the Mesopotamian kingdoms under his rule. It was about 2119 B.C. that he attacked Zembya, king of Isin; the latter summoned the Elamites to his aid and in one of the battles that followed Sin-idinnam lost his life. Then followed three short reigns, Sin-iribum or Sin-eribam, 2119–2117 B.C., Sin-ikishan or Sin-iqishan, 2117–2112 B.C., and Silli-Adad, 2112–2111 B.C., while an unknown king was reigning at Isin from 2118 to 2113 B.C.

Then a new king, Ur-Azag or Ur-dukugu, ascended the throne of Isin, and it appears that he kept up the alliance with Elam, for in 2111 B.C. Kutur-mabuk or Kudur-mabug, king of that land, attacked and defeated Silli-Adad, and placed his son Warad-Sin on the throne of Larsa, which he held till his death in 2099 B.C.

Ur-Azag was succeeded in 2109 B.C. by Sin-Magir, who ruled that state until 2098 B.C., while a year earlier Rim-Sin I succeeded his brother Warad-Sin as king of Larsa. Rim-Sin seems to have been a powerful monarch and he had the support of Elam, his father's kingdom. Still he left Isin in peace for a while. Sin-Magir had been succeeded by Damik-ilishu, who ruled that city, apparently peacefully, for nearly thirty years; but in 2069 B.C. Rim-Sin attacked him, captured the city and added the whole kingdom of Isin to the realm of Larsa.

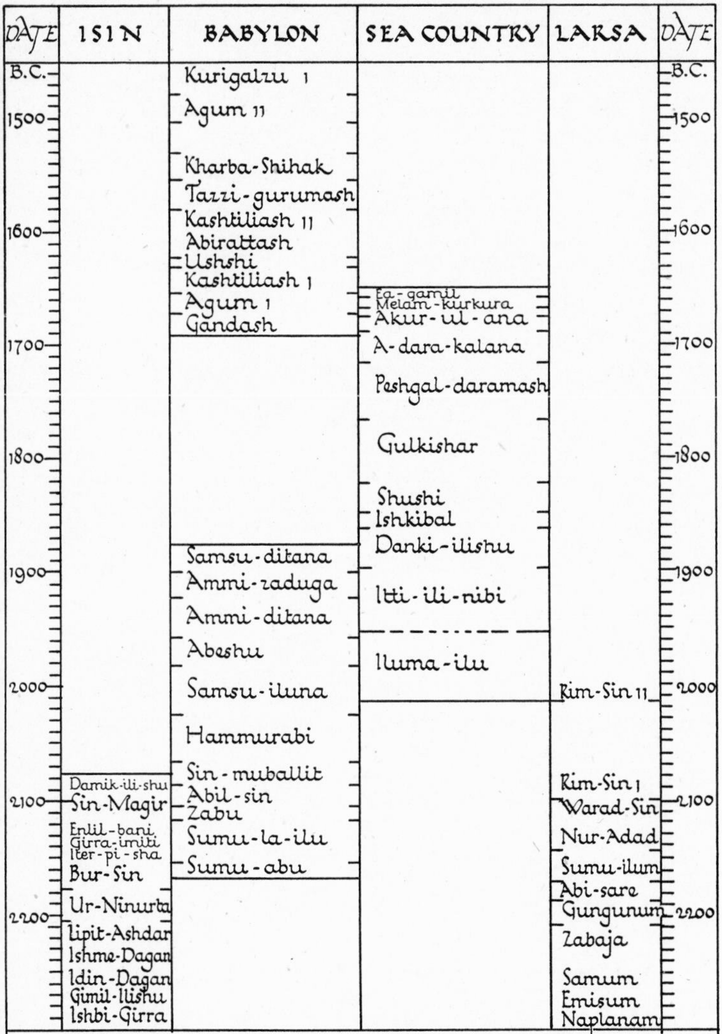

Chronological chart of the kings of Babylon, Isin and Larsa

DATE B.C.	ISIN	BABYLON	SEA COUNTRY	LARSA	DATE B.C.
		Kurigalzu 1			
1500		Agum 11			1500
		Kharba-Shihak			
1600		Tazzi-gurumash			1600
		Kashtiliash 11			
		Abirattash			
		Ushshi			
		Kashtiliash 1	Ea-gamil		
		Agum 1	Melam-Kurkura		
		Gandash	Akur-ul-ana		
1700			A-dara-kalana		1700
			Peshgal-daramash		
1800			Gulkishar		1800
			Shushi		
			Ishkibal		
			Danki-ilishu		
1900		Samsu-ditana			1900
		Ammi-zaduga	Itti-ili-nibi		
		Ammi-ditana			
		Abeshu	Iluma-ilu		
2000		Samsu-iluna		Rim-Sin 11	2000
		Hammurabi			
		Sin-muballit		Rim-Sin 1	
2100	Damik-ili-shu / Sin-Magir	Abil-sin / Zabu		Warad-Sin	2100
	Enlil-bani / Girra-imiti / Iter-pi-sha / Bur-Sin	Sumu-la-ilu		Nur-Adad	
		Sumu-abu		Sumu-ilum	
2200	Ur-Ninurta			Abi-sare / Gungunum	2200
	Lipit-Ashdar			Zabaja	
	Ishme-Dagan			Samum	
	Idin-Dagan			Emisum	
	Gimil-Ilishu			Naplanam	
	Ishbi-Girra				

Fig. 59. Chronological chart of the kings of Babylon, Isin and Larsa.

Note. The chart reads, in order of time, from the bottom upwards

Hammurabi, a young man, ascended the throne of Babylon in 2067 B.C., and lost no time in putting his kingdom in order. His first task was to organize his forces and to repair his city's fortifications. This done, in 2061 B.C. he marched his army southwards and wrested Erech and Isin from the hands of Rim-Sin; four years later he took several other cities from the kingdom of Larsa. These two expeditions were all that Hammurabi undertook during the first twenty-nine years of his reign, for he was busy at Babylon, building temples and setting up thrones for its deities, as well as fortifying some of the neighbouring towns. In 2038 B.C. he came into conflict with the forces of Elam, which was allied to Rim-Sin, and the following year he raided the southern territory and captured Rim-Sin himself. In the next year he followed this up with another expedition that resulted in the conquest of the remaining parts of the kingdom of Larsa. Hammurabi was now monarch of the whole of Mesopotamia, with Assyria, in its upper reaches, as a dependent province. Only Elam, on the Persian border, was independent, while the hill tribes to the north did not acknowledge his sway and often gave trouble on the border. The rest of his reign was taken up with rebuilding temples and constructing irrigation canals, though occasionally he had to send punitive expeditions to drive off the mountain tribes of the north. He died in 2024 B.C., after a reign of forty-three years.

Hammurabi was not only a great general but an able and wise administrator, and is best known from the code of laws called by his name. This was inscribed on a block of black diorite, found in 1901 by de Morgan at Susa. This code consists not so much of new enactments as of earlier laws, mainly of the Sumerians, but some of them, it would seem, of the Semitic Babylonians. The penalties for offences imposed by these laws seem to have been excessively severe, but, to judge from decisions recorded on contemporary tablets, these were rarely enforced. It is curious that the most savage punishments were reserved for the *amelu* or nobles, who were, it may be presumed, Semitic Babylonians, the descendants of the invading Amurru; on the other hand breaches of the law committed by the *mushkinu* or ordinary citizens, presumably the Sumerians and Akkadians, were usually settled by the infliction of fines. This distinction enables us to discriminate between the mental outlook of the Amurru and of the mixed peoples that they had conquered.

Besides these two classes of people, the *amelu* and the *mushkinu*, there were numerous slaves, whose status was quite different from either. These were, for the most part, captives taken in battle, or their descendants, though the *mushkinu* were liable to be degraded to a state of slavery for certain crimes.

Each city was governed by a council of elders or notables, presided over by a mayor known as a *rabianu*. There were judges of various degrees, appointed by the king, and an extensive civil service as well as a police force, all under the immediate direction of the monarch. From the laws we gather that arable land was held in individual ownership, but that pasturage was on common lands on the waste beyond. In some regions such pastures, and indeed arable lands as well, were held in common by tribes, presumably lately arrived from the desert.

While monogamy was the rule, in so far as only one wife was recognized as the mistress of the house, such men as could afford it had a number of concubines or wives of lower status. Divorce was easy on the part of the husband, for he had only to declare his wish and to return the dowry that he had received with the wife that he was divorcing; on the other hand it was far from easy for a wife to obtain release under any circumstances. All sons, as a rule, inherited equal portions of their father's estate. Daughters were dowered on marriage, but if unmarried at their father's death received an allowance from their brothers. The widow had an equal share with the sons of the husband's estate and kept her dower as well; the former of these she had to surrender on remarriage. If a wife died childless, her husband was required to return to her family the dower that he had received at her marriage. The dead were buried in two large jars, placed mouth to mouth, but about this time a new form of burial came into use, in which the body was placed in a large clay sarcophagus shaped like a bath-tub.

At the death of Hammurabi in 2024 B.C., he was succeeded by his son Samsu-iluna, who was a very different type of man. He seems to have been an indifferent general, a weak administrator and one who soon became unpopular with his subjects. The first eight years of his reign were uneventful, and his time was spent in digging fresh irrigation channels and in erecting statues to the numerous deities who had temples in his cities.

In 2016 B.C. his northern frontiers were raided by some hardy mountaineers from the Zagros range, who were known as Kassites, and of whom we shall hear more a few centuries later. A punitive expedition was sent to restore order, but the king was evidently unpopular, for the next year the Sumerian cities near the Persian Gulf revolted under the leadership of Rim-Sin II, an Elamite, who was probably the son of the Rim-Sin who had been deposed by Hammurabi from the throne of Larsa. Samsu-iluna led an expedition against these rebellious cities, suppressed the revolt, burned Rim-Sin alive in his palace at Larsa, and destroyed the fortifications of Erech and Ur. This last act was unwise, for in the desert to the south wandered nomad tribes ever ready to raid the cities on their borders.

Iluma-ilu, a chief of one of these tribes, took this opportunity, and in 2014 B.C. raided the lands of the Sumerians. Samsu-iluna was either unable or unwilling to defend them, and the cities again rose in revolt, which was with difficulty suppressed

in 2011 B.C. It would seem that the cities then threw in their
lot with the desert tribes, for Iluma-ilu appears to have occupied
all the lands at the mouths of the rivers, while Samsu-iluna

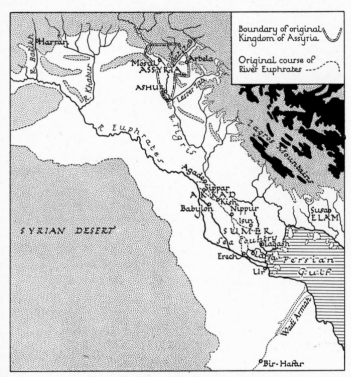

FIG. 60. Map of Babylonia and Assyria.

withdrew his forces and began to erect defences at Sippar. In
2005 B.C. another revolt took place, this time, it would seem,
led by Iluma-ilu, and the king of Babylon was unable to repress
it. The southern tribes continued to advance, and in 2001 B.C.
Samsu-iluna withdrew his line of defence to Kish and Nippur,

where he hastily erected fortifications. These, however, were of no avail, for in 1996 B.C. Ilumi-ilu captured Nippur, and consolidated all his possessions between that city and the Persian Gulf into a kingdom known as the Sea Country. Little territory was now left to Babylon, and when in 1988 B.C. the cities of Akkad revolted, Samsu-iluna had lost nearly all his kingdom but his capital of Babylon. In less than forty years the great kingdom of Hammurabi had melted away, owing to the incompetence of his son, who died in 1986 B.C.

Abeshu', the son of Samsu-iluna, who succeeded to the throne of Babylon, made an attempt to stem the invasion, but with little success. He tried to dam the Tigris in such a way that the whole of the country round Nippur should become flooded, but this scheme seems to have failed to achieve its object, for the Sea Country, now under the rule of Itti-ili-nibi, remained unimpaired. Nevertheless Nippur, up till now a city of great importance, declined rapidly in influence. Until his death in 1958 B.C. Abeshu' seems to have been content to remain monarch of his much-reduced dominions, which his son Ammi-ditana did nothing to increase until towards the closing years of his reign.

Ammi-ditana was succeeded in 1921 B.C. by his son Ammi-zaduga, in whose reign was made that observation on the occultation of Venus which has made it possible to date this period with accuracy. For the first ten years of his reign he did nothing to recover his lost territories, but in 1911 B.C. he led an expedition to the Persian Gulf, and the following year he destroyed a wall that had been built by Damki-ilishu, who was then king of the Sea Country, and erected a fort at the mouth of the Euphrates. This, however, seems to have had little effect, and on his death in 1900 B.C. it was a much restricted kingdom that he left to his son Samsu-ditana. This monarch seems to have been no more competent than his predecessors, for we hear of no attempts on his part to recover the kingdom of Hammurabi. The tribes of the desert and the mountain were again restless and invading his borders, and in 1870 B.C. a new power entered the scene of conflict. That year the Hittites, a people from Asia Minor, of whom we shall hear more presently, came down the Euphrates, captured Babylon, and brought the First Dynasty of that city to an end.

The Hittites did not stay to consolidate their conquest but retired again to their own country, carrying with them much booty from the stores of Babylon, and for nearly a century the documents from Mesopotamia are silent. The kings of the Sea Country were illiterate and left no monuments, and only the names of a few of their kings have come down to us. Ishkibal was reigning there about 1863 B.C., Shushi about 1848 B.C., and Gulkishar about 1821 B.C.; Peshgal-daramash, a son of the preceding king, was ruling the Sea Country about 1766 B.C. and had been succeeded by his son A-dara-kalama about 1716 B.C. Beyond the names of these monarchs we know little or nothing, and still less about the rest of Mesopotamia. The whole land seems to have become ravaged by wild mountain or desert tribes, the Kharrians from the north, the Kassites from the Zagros mountains, and perhaps other nomad tribes from the Syrian desert. At length in 1670 B.C. Gandash, a Kassite chief, made himself king in Babylon, thus founding the Kassite or Second Babylonian Dynasty.

We must now turn our attention to Assyria, to which reference has already been made, but which at this time was a country of little importance. It lay for the most part east of the Tigris above the junction with that river of the Lesser Zab, and extended as far upstream as Mosul, or a trifle beyond, and up to the foot-hills of the Zagros range as far as Arbela. On the west of the Tigris it extended little, if at all, beyond the immediate valley of that river. Its chief town, from which the country took its name, was Ashur or Asshur, spelt in earlier times Ashir and occasionally A-usar.

This district was originally part of a larger area known as Subartu, inhabited by the people of Su, who with the people of Gu, their neighbours on the south-east, had caused so much trouble to the kings of Agade. These people of Su were known in later times as Shubaraeans, and are usually written of to-day as Subaraeans. They spoke a language believed to be distantly related to the speech of the Elamites and to some of those strange tongues that are still spoken in a few of the valleys of the Caucasus. We have evidence from documents, dating from the time of the First Babylonian Dynasty, that there were fair individuals among the Subaraeans and among the people of Gu as well, for such fair people were at that time in great demand in Babylon as slaves. We may feel fairly certain, then, as we have already suspected, that there was a certain number of Nordic steppe-folk among both populations.

Recent excavations on the site of Asshur have shown that as early as the time of Entemena, king of Lagash about 2950 B.C., the city had come under Sumerian influences. Indeed it seems likely that the city was founded by people from Sumer, for the Subaraeans, like the people of Gu, were probably not city dwellers. Most of the objects found in the lower layers on this site are of definitely Sumerian type, though no inscriptions were found to throw any light upon its history. There were, however, a few pots and cult objects of quite different form, more nearly resembling some found in various places in Asia Minor; these may have arrived by way of trade, or may in some cases be the products of native Subaraean workmanship.

Some little time before the accession of Sargon to the throne of Agade in 2752 B.C., but at a date which cannot yet be determined with accuracy, the city of Asshur and the surrounding district were conquered by a people speaking a Semitic tongue, who according to Sidney Smith came from some region between the Tigris and the Euphrates, just south of the mountains, somewhere, that is to say, in the neighbourhood of the valleys of the Khabur and the Balikh and not far from the modern town of Harran. In spite of their Semitic speech, their portraits, or to be more accurate, those of their descendants, show them to have been mainly of the Armenoid or eastern Alpine type.

Assyria seems to have been conquered by Sargon of Agade early in his reign; at his death it recovered its independence for a while, but was reconquered later by Naram-Sin. It remained a dependence of Agade until the reign of Shargalisharri, after which, it is believed, it fell under the domination of the kings of Gutium, the people of Gu mentioned above.

At the fall of the dynasty of

FIG. 61. Terra-cotta vase in the anthropomorphic style from Asshur (after Andrae).

Gutium in 2468 B.C. Assyria seems to have become independent, for about that time we hear of two kings, Ushpia and Kikia, who are thought to have been Subaraeans, though, according to Sidney Smith, on insufficient evidence. A third king, Ititi, lived about the same time. Assyria came, however, under the rule of the Third Dynasty of Ur, for under the third king of that dynasty, Bur-Sin, or Pur-Sin, who reigned from 2345 to 2337 B.C., Zariku or Zariqu, governor of Asshur under that monarch, erected in the city a temple to Belti-ekallim, 'for the life of his sovereign of Ur'.

For some time after this the records of Assyria are silent, and we are left in uncertainty whether either of the rival kingdoms of Isin and Larsa succeeded in bringing that country under their sway. In a document dating from about 800 B.C. we hear of a king, Enlil-kapkapu, who is thought to have reigned in Asshur about 2200 B.C., though some authorities doubt his existence. But soon after this Puzur-Ashir I, who styled himself 'tenant farmer of the district of Ashur', established himself firmly on the throne; he is known to have been a contemporary of Ur-Ninurta, king of Isin between 2207 and 2179 B.C. We know little of the doings of this king and even less about those of his son and successor, Shalim-Akhum, but the son of the latter, who followed, seems to have been engaged in helping the Akkadian and Sumerian cities to retain their independence when threatened by Sumu-abu of Babylon.

Of the kings that followed in succession from father to son, Irishum I, Ikunum I, and Sharru-kin I, we know little more, except that the last-named was reigning about 2150 B.C., and styled himself 'tenant-farmer of the god Ashur'. During the reigns of these three monarchs Assyria seems to have been prospering and to have been carrying on extensive trade with Asia Minor.

After the death of Sharru-kin, who is often called Sargon, a king of a new line arose. This was Puzur-Ashir II, who was succeeded by Akhi-Ashir. The latter had not long been on the throne when Kutur-Mabuk or Kudur-Mabug, originally an Elamite prince of Emutbal or Yamutbal, but who had for some time been the ruler of the whole of the Elamite territory, attacked Assyria. In 2111 B.C. he had conquered the kingdom of Larsa, over which he had placed his son Warad-Sin, who was succeeded in 2099 B.C. by his brother Rim-Sin. The latter had been king of Larsa for some years before he completely conquered the kingdom of Isin in 2069 B.C., and it seems to have been about this time that his father defeated the Assyrians and added their territory to the kingdom of Larsa. Assyria remained part of this kingdom until its conquest in 2037 B.C. by Hammurabi, who placed on the throne Shamshi-Adad I, who seems to have held his kingdom as a dependence of Babylon.

Shamshi-Adad I was the son of Irikapkapu and seems to have come from the west, whence the original Assyrians had at an earlier time arrived. He added considerably to the Assyrian kingdom; first he included all his original possessions, which seem to have lain in the Harran district, and ultimately extended his dominions to the shore of the Mediterranean. He was succeeded by his son Ishme-Dagan I, of whom little is known, and then by two others, the second of whom, Rimush, brought the line of Shamshi-Adad to an end. After this, rival dynasties ruled in Assyria for a few years, four kings in one and three in the other; then the kingdom was united by Shi-Ninua, whose successor, Sharma-Adad II, was reigning when Gandash, the Kassite, ascended the throne of Babylon.

We cannot close this chapter without making some reference to Abram, who is believed to have lived about this time. In the Book of Genesis, Abram is described as a Hebrew, and there has been much speculation as to the real meaning of this word. The name occurs on more than one occasion, as Khabirai in the time of Rim-Sin, and as Khabiru at a later date in a Hittite document, and again in the same form in an Egyptian inscription of the fourteenth century B.C. This word has been variously interpreted, as 'robbers' in the Egyptian instance and as 'mercenaries' in the two other cases.

Sidney Smith has recently made the interesting suggestion that the earliest form Khabiru means the men from the town or district of Khabir, while an Aramaic document of the late seventh century mentions a town Khafiru, lying in the desert off the extreme south of Babylonia, while a later writer describes this place as lying west of Basra. It seems to have been the district around the town of Bir-Hafar, which lies at the head of the Wadi Armah, 180 miles south-west of Basra on a trade route leading towards Mecca.

Be this as it may, we learn from the Book of Genesis that Abram with his father Terah settled in the city of Ur, but left it some years later and migrated northwards to the district around Haran, where Terah died. It has sometimes been thought that this departure occurred at the fall of the Third Dynasty of Ur in 2301 B.C., but the reference to the Khabirai, who were fighting among the forces of Rim-Sin, suggests that they did not leave until the downfall of Rim-Sin's kingdom in 2036 B.C.

From Haran Abram went to Sichem in Canaan and thence to Bethel, following a route that was afterwards superseded by the road along the coastal plain to Esdraelon, when horse traffic had come into use. After a visit to Egypt, where he was hospitably treated by the king, he returned again to Bethel. It was soon after this time that, according to the Book of Genesis, Chedor-laomer, king of Elam, with Amraphael, king of Shinar, Arioch, king of Ellasar, and Tidal, king of the Goim or hordes, set out to put down a revolt in the Jordan valley. In doing this they took as prisoner Lot, the nephew of Abram, and the patriarch set out to rescue his relation, and accomplished this successfully.

Attempts have been made to identify these four kings, Amraphael with Hammurabi, which is quite possible, Arioch with Warad-Sin, whose name in Sumerian reads Eri-aku, and Tidal with Dudkhalis, a king of the Hittites. There are, however, difficulties in the way of these identifications. It is agreed that Amraphael may be Hammurabi, but Chedor-laomer, though a quite possible Elamite name in the form of Kudur-Lagomal, is not known as a king of Elam, while Kudur-mabug occupied that throne during the greater part if not all of the reign of Hammurabi. Warad-Sin had died long before Hammurabi succeeded to the throne, and preceded Rim-Sin, under whom the Khabirai are said to have served. Lastly, though there was a Dudkhalis or Tudkhalis, king of the Hittites, at a much later date, we have no reason for supposing that there was such a king at this time.

Dr. S. A. Cook, while admitting that some, if not all, of these names may be those of real individuals, believes that the account of this campaign was compiled in the fifth century B.C. On the other hand, Mr. Campbell Thompson cites a tablet on which Dr. Pinches discovered the names 'Eri-A-KU, Ku-dur-ku-ku-mal, king of E-la . . . and Tu-ud-khul-a, son of Gaz . . .', and says that 'we cannot dismiss the possibility of the Elamites having raided Syria'. Sidney Smith has stated more recently that the question is incapable of solution on the evidence at present available.

BOOKS

Cambridge Ancient History, vol. i (Cambridge, 1923).
DELAPORTE, L. *Mesopotamia* (London, 1925).
KING, L. W. *A History of Babylon* (London, 1915).
SMITH, SIDNEY. *Early History of Assyria* (London, 1928).

II

Asia Minor, Turkistan, and China

A NEW power was at this time arising in Asia Minor; this was the empire of the Hittites, who brought to an end the rule of the First Babylonian Dynasty. The Khatti or Hatti, as they are called in contemporary documents, were one of a number of kindred tribes occupying large parts of Asia Minor and neighbouring regions. Large numbers of clay tablets have been found at Boghaz Keui in the Halys basin, written in cuneiform script, borrowed from Sumerian traders, who had settled in those parts; these, though written some centuries later than the time with which we are dealing, throw considerable light on the earlier history and affinities of the inhabitants of this region. From these tablets we gather that there were several closely allied tribes, speaking cognate languages of a type that is called Asianic, while in one of these dialects, that known as Kanesian, occur features that bear some resemblance to those of certain Indo-European tongues. Further than this, there are references to a number of deities whose names closely resemble those of gods of the Indian and Greek pantheons. The names of many of their kings and leading personages have also an Indo-European appearance. From this it is believed that the Khatti and allied tribes were a people of the Armenoid or eastern Alpine type, who originally spoke an Asianic language, but that at some time they were conquered by a relatively small group of Indo-European-speaking warriors, who were, as we believe, nomad Nordic people from the steppes of south Russia and Turkistan. In this connexion it is well to note that on a seal impression from Cappadocia, where the Hittites lived, dating from between 2100 and 1900 B.C., is figured a four-horsed chariot. The Kanesian dialect, it is believed, was the official tongue of the Hittite empire, and was that spoken by these Nordic conquerors after they had learned the language of their subjects.

The first mention that we have of the Hittites is in a document recording the conquests of Naram-Sin, king of Agade between 2673 and 2633 B.C. From this we learn that, among many kings defeated by this monarch, one was Pamba, king of the Khatti. We are not given any information as to the region in which this tribe then dwelt, but, since a bas-relief of a standing figure of Naram-Sin was found some years ago in the village of Pir-Hussein, about twenty miles north-east of Diabekr, it is possible that at this time the Khatti were living in the western half of the upper basin of the Tigris.

The next reference to these people is somewhat obscure. A tablet found at Boghaz Keui contains an inscription that is believed to date from shortly after the time of Naram-Sin. In this a certain Anittas, who describes himself as the great king,

Fig. 62. Standing figure of Naram-Sin, found at Pir-Hussein.

states that he took the city of Khattusas or Khattushash from Biyustis. Anittas is said to have been a son of Bitkhanas, king of Kussar or Kushar, a town at the south-east of Lake Tatta, known in later days as Garsaüra, and believed to have been the original home of the Hittites. Kattusas, the modern Boghaz Keui, was in later days the capital of the Hittite Empire, and so it has been thought that Biyustis was a Hittite king. This, of course, may be so, but the interpretation of this document is not easy.

We learn more from another tablet from the same site, containing an inscription of Telibinus or Telibinush, who seems to have been king of the Khatti soon after 1800 B.C. He relates the whole history of the kingdom from the time of Labarnas or Tabarnas, his predecessor, until his accession to the throne. He speaks of Labarnas as if he were the first king, and his name and those of all the other kings and nobles mentioned seem to be of Indo-European type; we may conjecture, therefore, that Labarnas was the first of the nomad Nordics to establish his rule over the Khatti. It is noticeable in this tablet that the names of queens occur with almost as great frequency as those of kings, and we find the same in other tablets, where the queen's name often precedes that of her husband when they occur together. From this it seems likely that originally descent had followed the female line, and that the Nordic conquerors, with whom patrilinear succession was the rule, made a practice of marrying the royal heiress of the native line.

From the tablet of Telibinus it would appear that Labarnas became king of the Khatti some little time before 1900 B.C. and married Tawannannas, who we suspect was the heiress of a preceding sovereign. It is uncertain whether he had his capital at Khattusas, but early in his reign he was occupying the steppe region of Lycaonia, to the south-east of Iconium, including the cities of Khubisna and Tuwanuwa, afterwards known as Cybistra and Tyana. After consolidating his empire in the centre of Asia Minor, he extended it southwards as far as the sea; then he returned to his capital, but allowed some of his sons and nobles to settle in the lands he had conquered.

He was succeeded in due course by his son Khattusilis, who mustered all his sons, brothers, and relations, and with their aid extended his dominion. He seems to have conquered the greater part of north Syria, which he placed under the command of his sons and nobles, while he returned to Asia Minor. Twice

the newly annexed territories revolted, and on the second
occasion he seems to have gone in person to put down the
rebellion, but was killed at Aleppo.

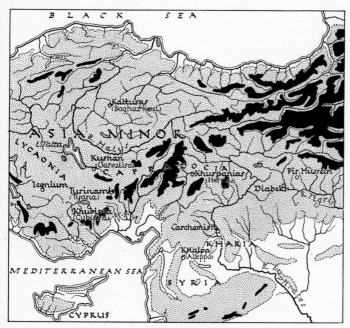

FIG. 63. Map of the Hittite Empire.

He was succeeded by his son Murshilis or Mursilis, who had
his capital at Khattusas; he married first of all Kattusis and
afterwards Kharabsilis, who had been the wife of Alluwamnas,
apparently the king of some conquered city. One of his first
acts was to lead an expedition to Khalpa, the modern Aleppo,
to avenge the death of his father, and shortly afterwards in
1870 B.C. he marched to Carchemish, descended the Euphrates,
sacked Babylon and brought to an end the First Dynasty of

that city. After that he had an encounter with the Kharrians, of whom more will be said later, before returning with his booty to Khattusas.

It would seem that, not long after his return to his capital, Mursilis fell victim to a palace plot. Two of the officers of his household, Zidantas and Khantilis, his cup-bearer, conspired against him and murdered him. Then Khantilis ascended the throne after marrying Kharabsilis, the widow of the dead king, while Zidantas married Iyáyas, the daughter of the usurper. Having first fortified Khattusas, Khantilis marched with his army to Khurpanias, the later Herpa, and thence over the mountains to Carchemish and so on to Tegarama, which seems to have lain some miles to the east. After that some disaster seems to have occurred, for the tablet continues 'then the gods avenged the blood of Mursilis'; Sayce believes that Khantilis was defeated by the Kharrians, who killed some of his sons and the queen of Sukzia, possibly the wife of one of them. After having avenged these murders, Khantilis, having grown old, abdicated in favour of his son Bisenis or Kassenis, but the ambitions of Zidantas, his former co-conspirator and son-in-law, were not satisfied; he murdered Bisenis, his sons and his principal servants, and usurped the throne. He was not, however, to be left long in possession of his ill-gained power, for he quarrelled with his son Ammunas, who slew his father and ascended the throne, after which, so the tablet says, there was a famine to avenge the deed.

The accession of Ammunas was followed by a general revolt of the subject peoples; this the king endeavoured to quell, but in vain. After his death his son Zûrus, the captain of the body-guard of spearmen, seems to have murdered one of his brothers, and for a time there was constant strife in the palace, till at length Telibinus, who came from Turmitta, north of Khattusas, marched on the capital and took it.

Some authorities consider that Telibinus founded a new dynasty, but he expressly states that he ascended the throne of his father, who is elsewhere stated to have been Khuzzias. Telibinus makes a point of mentioning that he took Istapariyas

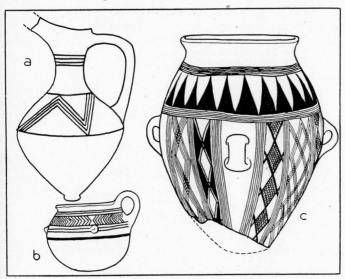

FIG. 64. Early Hittite pottery from: *a.* and *b.* the Musée Guimet, Paris; *c.* the Antiquarium, Berlin.

as his first wife. He seems to have reconquered all the cities that formerly belonged to the Hittite Empire, and to have ruled them wisely. He made his younger sons regents in Carchemish, Aleppo, and elsewhere, and was in due course succeeded by his son Mursilis II.

Little as yet can be said about the material civilization of the Hittites at this time. Numerous specimens of their pottery are possessed by the principal national museums, but as these have, for the most part, been purchased from traders, their exact period is unknown, though it is believed that most of them must be attributed to a much later date. Hrozny has recently brought back some pots from the mound of Kültepe at Kara Euyuk, which are probably somewhat earlier than the time of Labarnas, while a pair in the Musée Guimet in Paris, and a vase in the Antiquarium in Berlin, appear from their style to be early, and may date from this time.

We must now consider how these conquerors of the Hittite tribes reached the central plain of Asia Minor. In our last volume we gave reasons for believing that certain nomad pastoral people, of Nordic type and of Aryan or Indo-European speech, left the grasslands of south Russia and Turkistan about 2600 b.c., and spread in every direction. We traced in some detail their movements to the north and west, we suggested that they reached Thessaly by way of Bulgaria, and we suspected their identity with the people of Su and Gu, who dwelt in the foot-hills of the Zagros mountains, and were giving trouble to the kings of Agade as early as the time of Sargon.

Later on we shall again meet with other peoples who seem to have been ruled by kings and aristocracies of these men of the northern steppe; two have been mentioned already, the Kharrians and the Kassites, who eventually established themselves in Babylon. All this seems to show that these mobile adventurers, all the more mobile because they had recently acquired increased power over and use of the horse, had reached the Tigris basin from the east or north-east. If we are right in believing that they came from the northern steppe, we can have little doubt that they passed through the opening between the Kopet Dagh range and the Hindu Kush, and travelled westwards and south-westwards across the Iranian plateau.

Dr. S. Prseworski has suggested that the ancestors of the Hittite monarchs reached the Anatolian plateau from the west, having crossed the Dardanelles and sacked the Second City of

Hissarlik on their way. They were, he believes, the vanguard of that movement which brought the Briges from Thrace or Macedonia as Phrygians into the north-west corner of Asia Minor. Most writers have believed that the advent of the Phrygians was many centuries later, though it is admitted that the date of this movement is uncertain. If, however, Labarnas, or one of his predecessors, destroyed Hissarlik on his way to the plain of Lycaonia, where we first hear of him, the destruction of Hissarlik II must be dated earlier than 1900 B.C., where it has lately been the custom to place it, for Labarnas must have been well established on the Hittite throne a quarter of a century before that date. Frankfort, too, is inclined to believe that Hissarlik was destroyed by Labarnas, or his immediate successor, but he would bring the destroyers from the east, i.e. after Labarnas had established himself on the Hittite throne, which creates no difficulty in the chronology.

In favour of the approach from Europe is the fact that in the Kanesian tongue Hrozny recognizes features that occur again in Italic and Celtic dialects, but on the other hand he notices, too, resemblances to Tocharian, a language found later in central Asia, while the names of the Hittite deities resemble in form those mentioned in the Vedas more closely than their Greek counterparts. Until more systematic excavation has been carried out on a number of early Hittite sites, the question must remain undecided, but on the evidence at present available, the balance of probability seems to be in favour of the arrival of these conquerors from the east.

The Kharrians or Khurri, to whom reference has more than once been made, were a branch of the Subaraean people, living originally in the district known as Kharia, which lies at the foot of the mountains, where the Euphrates debouches on to the plain. Later on they occupied the highland region between the Euphrates and Lake Van. Like the Subaraeans, they seem to have been a people of the mountain region of west Persia, allied to the Elamites, and speaking a Caucasic tongue, but before the period with which we are dealing they had come under the rule of Nordic chiefs of Indo-European speech.

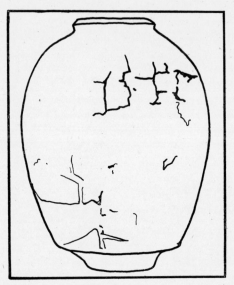

Fig. 65. Pot from the South Kurgan at Anau in Turkistan.

These chiefs seem to have belonged to the Indo-Iranian group of these people, and the names of their deities closely resemble those worshipped by the Indians and Persians in early times, for in a treaty of a later date we find the names of Indar (Indra), Mitra (Mithra), Varuna, and the Nasatianna twins. That they had tamed the horse before this date is clear from the remains that have been found of a work in their language on chariot-racing or horse-training, in which a number of technical terms in Sanskrit have been found. They are often inaccurately termed Mitannians, because in later times some of them founded the kingdom of Mitanni.

In previous volumes of this series we have described two mounds or kurgans near Anau in Turkistan, explored some years ago by Pumpelly, and in our fourth volume we suggested that the settlement on the north Kurgan was abandoned about 2750 B.C., either owing to its destruction by the nomads of the steppe, or because the waters from the mountains behind failed to reach so far into the plain and so to be available for irrigating the crops grown by the inhabitants.

It was probably about 2000 B.C., or perhaps a little earlier, that a new village was established some little way to the south of the former site, and so nearer to the source of the water supply. This settlement is known as the south Kurgan. Among the remains found in the lower part of this mound, laid down during the period known as Anau III, are implements of copper in abundance, occasionally containing a low percentage of tin; these include daggers, sickles, lance-heads, and arrow-heads. Some of these have been intentionally alloyed with lead. Stone arrow-heads were still in use, as well as some of obsidian, which must have been imported, probably from Armenia.

The pottery was in many ways different from that found in the north Kurgan, both in form and decoration. It was made with a wheel and fired in well-constructed kilns, some of which have been found. Very little of it was decorated with painted designs, and such as there were show a decided falling-off in the technique; a few of the pots had incised ornament. Some female figurines of earthenware were found in this mound and a few of bulls or cows.

The houses were built of sun-dried bricks and their doors had pivotal hinges. The inhabitants had a curious custom of burying their children in a contracted position under the floors of their houses. Near the top of the deposit was found a three-faced seal. It is difficult to give dates with any approach to accuracy for the foundation or the abandonment of this settlement, and the conjectures of different writers vary considerably. Dr. Hubert Schmidt, who excavated the mound for Mr.

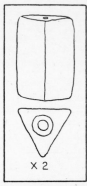

FIG. 66. Three-faced seal from the South Kurgan at Anau in Turkistan.

Pumpelly, was inclined to date the three-faced seal at about 1500 B.C., and this lay near the top of the deposit.

The scholars of a generation ago, in reaction against some older uncritical work, were inclined to disregard legendary history, but Schliemann and Dörpfeld had just been demonstrating its essential value for Troy, and Evans was about to show how much of it was true for Crete. In previous volumes, especially in volumes iii and iv, we have ventured to go rather beyond accepted opinion in suggesting the possible value of the legendary history of Mesopotamia, and we think it useful to adopt the same attitude with reference to China, especially since the discoveries of Andersson and Arne, discussed in volume v, and marked + on the map on page 147.

We mentioned in our last volume, *The Steppe and the Sown*, that according to the Shu King, the classical history of China, the first emperor of that country, Yao, ascended the throne in 2357 B.C. The centre of his kingdom lay near the junction of the Wei-ho with the Hwang-ho, but during his time his dominions are said to have been considerably extended, so that before his death, according to Confucius, his empire included all the lower Yangtze basin, the whole of the plain as far north as Peking and as far west as the extremity of the Shantung peninsula. According to the Chinese sage, Yao was 'all-informed, intelligent, accomplished, and thoughtful', and ruled the 'black-haired race' with godlike instinct. It was in 2293 B.C., according to the Chinese history, that his empire suffered from a terrible inundation, due to one of the periodic floods caused

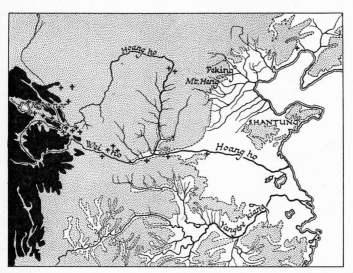

Fig. 67. Map of China.

by the Hwang-ho, so often called 'China's Sorrow'. Yao assembled his leading men and implored them to find some one to control the flood. Kwan was selected as suitable for this work, but laboured for nine years without succeeding in draining off the waters. Yao was then advised to employ Shun, a man of the people, who exiled Kwan and called upon Yu, Kwan's son, to help him in the task. Yu set to work deepening the bed of the river and cutting new channels, so that the waters were drained away.

Yao died in 2258 B.C., and Shun was chosen to succeed him,

and reigned until 2206 B.C., when he was succeeded by Yu, who is considered as the first emperor of the Hsia Dynasty. He is said to have reorganized his empire, dividing it into nine provinces instead of eleven, and when he died an inscription to his memory was carved upon a rock on Mount Heng. Little is known, at any rate to their credit, of the acts of Yu's sixteen successors; as so often happens, there was a steady decline from the virtues and abilities of the founder of the dynasty. The last of the line, Chieh Kwei, was the most notorious of them all, so much so that his infamy became proverbial. His conduct was so outrageous that the people rose in revolt under T'ang, who dethroned the wicked emperor in 1766 B.C., and placed himself upon the throne as the first monarch of the Yin Dynasty.

Little is known of the civilization of this period beyond the fact that the people grew grain and kept cattle, made pottery and had become expert in casting bronze. The population seems to have been organized on a tribal basis under patriarchal rule, while the provinces were governed by nobles, who held their lands on some form of feudal tenure.

BOOKS

The Cambridge Ancient History, vols. i and ii (Cambridge, 1923 and 1924).
COWLEY, A. *The Hittites* (Schweich Lectures, 1918).
GARSTANG, J. *The Land of the Hittites* (London, 1910).
HALL, H. R. *Ancient History of the Near East* (London, 1920).
MESSERSCHMIDT, L. *The Hittites* (Ancient East Series, vi, 1903).
PUMPELLY, R. *Explorations in Turkistan* (Washington, 1905 and 1908).
SOOTHILL, W. E. *A History of China* (London, 1927).

12

The Middle Kingdom in Egypt

WE left Egypt in a turmoil, owing to the revolution and invasions that had led to the downfall of the Old Kingdom. We noted that two dynasties, the ninth and tenth, had been reigning successively at Heracleopolis and had driven the invaders out of Middle Egypt, but at the time that this chapter opens, about 2200 B.C., the invaders, both Libyans and Asiatics, were still in possession of the Delta, while in the remainder of the land the district governors, or nomarchs, held almost independent sway as feudal princes, only just acknowledging the suzerainty of the kings of Heracleopolis.

Among these feudal princes were the rulers at Hermonthis, near Thebes, in the extreme south, believed by Petrie to have been of Nubian extraction. They usually bore the name of Intef or Antef. At Siût was settled a rival family which supported the authority of the kings, while the Intefs in the south, though they defended the land from the incursions of the 'People of the bow', claimed almost independent power. One of these Intefs, a son of Ikui and probably a descendant of an earlier Intef, was styled the 'Keeper of the Door of the South'. He was not content with the great powers and privileges he already possessed, but rebelled against his lord at Heracleopolis and set up an independent state that stretched almost from the First Cataract as far north as Thebes. He was continuing his advance when the nomarch of Siût, ever faithful to his sovereign, brought two armies against him and arrested his conquests near Abydos, which the Thebans then termed 'the Door of the North'.

Intef was succeeded in due course by his son, who assumed

the name and dignity of a king about 2160 B.C. This monarch, known as Intef I, enlarged his kingdom to include Abydos and the whole of the Thinite nome, but was unable to extend it farther north owing to the opposition of the nomarch of Siût. He reigned for more than fifty years, when he was succeeded by his son Intef II, of whom little is known.

Intef II was succeeded about 2100 B.C. by Mentuhotep I, who is thought to have been his cousin, and several other monarchs of the same name ascended the throne in succession. The number of these kings is variously given as four or five. One of these, Moret believes the last, finally overthrew the power of the kings of Heracleopolis and brought the whole of Egypt again under one rule. During his reign, which seems to have lasted for thirty years, the wealth and prosperity of the land increased rapidly, and expeditions were again sent into the desert to obtain metals and precious stones. His vizier, Amenemhet, seems to have been governor of Thebes, which was becoming the most important city if not the actual capital, and after the death of the last Mentuhotep, in or about 2000 B.C., Amenemhet the vizier, or according to others a descendant of his bearing the same name, assumed regal power as first king of the Twelfth Dynasty with his capital at Thebes.

Amenemhet was not of royal blood, but, since some of his descendants claimed the first Intef as an ancestor, it seems possible that he, like many of his predecessors, had married a royal princess. He was a strong ruler and insisted that all should obey his laws. He found in the nomarchs a set of powerful hereditary princes, almost independent, and he proceeded to curtail their authority and to insist that they should govern their lands according to his just laws. While leaving them in possession of their hereditary estates, he made them hold their official lands at his pleasure; by this means, by frequently appointing the son of a nomarch to a like office in another nome, and by rewarding the good and dismissing the unjust, he effected considerable reforms. Thus the magistracies began to lose their

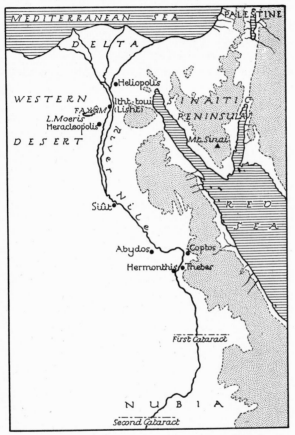

FIG. 68. Map of Egypt during the Middle Kingdom.

hereditary character, while on the walls of their tombs the nomarchs have left inscriptions claiming that they never ill-treated the peasants but always administered the law with justice. Although severe to the unworthy nomarchs, Amenemhet endeavoured to win the loyalty and affection of the remainder; for this purpose he arranged that their sons should be brought up at his court, where they were treated with great consideration.

Amenemhet seems to have been a native of Thebes, which had become the capital of Egypt during the latter part of the previous dynasty. He made the local god Amon the chief deity throughout Egypt, though, to appease the sun-worshippers of Heliopolis, he identified him with Re under the name of Amon-Re. Finding Thebes too remote for his capital, he erected a fortified city, called Itht-toui, 'the controller of the two lands', about thirty miles south of Cairo, near the modern village of Lisht, and from here he ruled the whole country.

During the first years of his reign he had to expel some foreigners from the Delta; this he did by carrying his troops down the Nile in a fleet of twenty river ships. His reign was otherwise peaceful, and he seems to have been popular with his nobles in spite of his severity to those whom he deemed unworthy of their office. Nevertheless towards the close of his reign an attempt was made upon his life, and soon afterwards, in 1980 B.C., he associated his son Senusret with him upon the throne. The two monarchs reigned jointly, the father dealing with domestic affairs, the son with foreign expeditions, and it was while the latter was absent conducting a punitive expedition against the Libyan tribes of the western desert that Amenemhet died in 1970 B.C.

Senusret I spent the greater part of his reign in enlarging the bounds of his kingdom, especially to the south and east. He conducted an expedition to Nubia early in his reign, and in 1962 B.C. sent his general Mentuhotep in command of another, which carried his dominions as far as the Second Cataract. The object of these expeditions, and of others into the eastern desert, was to secure supplies of gold, which was plentiful in Nubia and occurred also in the desert east of Coptos. These goldfields were worked soon afterwards, thereby increasing the wealth of the kingdom. In 1938 B.C. he took as co-regent his son Amenemhet, who succeeded him at his death in 1935 B.C.

Fig. 69. Mortuary boat of Senusret III, from his pyramid at Dashur.

Amenemhet II did nothing to extend the boundaries of his kingdom, though he reopened the turquoise and copper mines in the Sinaitic peninsula that had been worked under the kings of the Old Kingdom. At his death in 1903 B.C. he was succeeded by his son Senusret II, of whom little is known but that he died in 1887 B.C., when he was succeeded by his son Senusret III.

This king completed a canal to enable boats to ascend the First Cataract, and founded a number of stations in Nubia, where he settled many of the Egyptians. He fixed his boundary above the Second Cataract, north of which no negro was allowed to pass. This boundary he afterwards defended with two forts, so as to prevent negroes passing without a permit. He carried out many punitive expeditions to the south and east, both to keep the desert tribes in order and to enlarge his bounds; he also led an army into Palestine. The Cretans, known here at this time as Haunebu, were frequent visitors to Egypt, and vases of Kamares ware of the Second Middle Minoan period have been found in a tomb at Kahun. Towards the close of his life he associated his son with him on the throne, as his predecessors had done, and at his death in 1849 B.C. this son, Amenemhet, succeeded him.

Senusret III had been a man of resolute character, who had still further reduced the power of the feudal princes; much of his time had been spent in warlike expeditions beyond the limits of his kingdom. His successor, Amenemhet III, was of a more peaceful disposition and contented himself with organizing more completely the domains obtained by the efforts of his predecessors. He improved the approaches to the mines near Mount Sinai and elsewhere, sinking wells on the routes leading to them or cleaning out those sunk in earlier days. He carried out great improvements in the irrigation system and, with a view to controlling the supply of water, built great dams to regulate the ingress and egress of the water of the reservoir created by his predecessors in the Fayûm and known as Lake Moeris. He lived to a considerable age, continuing his good works, and died in 1801 B.C., when he was succeeded by his son Amenemhet IV, who had reigned with him for a short time.

The last of the Amenemhets seems to have lacked the sturdy character of his predecessors, for the prosperity of the land rapidly diminished during his reign. He left few monuments, so that we have but an imperfect picture of this time. His reign was short, for he died in 1792 B.C. leaving no son, and he was succeeded by the Princess Sebeknefrure, who may have been his daughter.

Queen Sebeknefrure endeavoured to resuscitate the fallen fortunes of Egypt, but without success, and after a four years' struggle married in 1788 B.C. Khutouire Ugafa, who in the

FIG. 70. Head of Amenemhet III, from a sphinx found at Tanis.

right of his wife ascended the throne as first monarch of the Thirteenth Dynasty. His succession was disputed by the people of Thebes, who set up as king a descendant of one of the earlier monarchs of the Twelfth Dynasty. Egypt was thus riven asunder, and at a later date a third independent kingdom arose in the Delta.

For the hundred years that followed the foundation of the Thirteenth Dynasty the monuments are too few in number to enable us to construct a consecutive story. From the Turin papyrus we learn that fourteen monarchs, all unimportant and with short reigns, succeeded Khutouire, after which Sebek-hotep I reunited the kingdom for a while. Then two kings called Sebekemsaf I and II, and perhaps a third king Upuautem-saf, ruled at Thebes alone, followed after an interval by Sebekhotep II and the brothers Menuazre, Neferhotep, and

Fig. 71. Diadem of a Twelfth Dynasty princess, found in her tomb at Dashur.

Sebekhotep III, who were reigning about 1690 B.C. It is clear that these brothers were men of the people and that the heredi-tary succession had failed. After this no further attempt was made for a while to unite the kingdom.

From information recently obtained in Palestine by Sir Flinders Petrie, it appears probable that at the close of the Twelfth Dynasty another horde of Asiatics settled in the eastern part of the Delta, where they established what is known as the Fifteenth Dynasty, and, at the fall of the Thirteenth Dynasty, these ruled over the whole land, being reckoned as the Sixteenth Dynasty. These were the well-known Hyksos or Shepherd Kings.

It is impossible within the limits of this volume to attempt a description of the civilization of Egypt during the time of the Twelfth Dynasty, or the Middle Kingdom as it is called, and readers desirous of learning more about this interesting period must refer to the volumes cited at the end of this chapter. It was the age in which sculpture, painting, woodcarving and jewelry reached their highest pitch of perfection,

FIG. 72. Coffin and mortuary furniture from a Twelfth Dynasty tomb.

but in most respects the material civilization of the people was not unlike that which had existed under the Old Kingdom. The only new element in that civilization was bronze, which came first into use at this time.

Egypt was still a self-contained land and imported little except timber, oil, and wine from Syria. These imports were paid for by the exportation of grain and of gold extracted by slaves from the Nubian mines. There was no great change in the life of the people, except that for the first time we notice the rise of a middle class between the nobles and the peasants, attached as serfs to the soil. This middle class had become educated, and provided not only the traders and the skilled artisans, but also the members of a civil service, which was considerably increased during the latter half of the Twelfth Dynasty.

Considerable changes had occurred in the funeral customs. The kings were still buried under pyramids, though some, like Senusret III, had a duplicate tomb cut in the rock. The nobles were all buried in rock-cut tombs opening out of the sloping face of the cliffs by the side of the valley. It is, however, in the furniture of these tombs that the greatest change is observed. The body was enclosed in a great wooden chest, painted to represent a human body and face, and with it were buried a number of wooden models, depicting the servants of the deceased engaged in the various occupations that they had followed in this world and were destined to follow in the next.

At this time, too, we find the first of those small figures, called *shauabti* or *ushabti*, which became more common in later periods and are met with so frequently in collections of Egyptian antiquities. Their name means 'answerers', and they were supposed to answer 'Here am I' whenever the deceased was called upon to do any manual labour in the next world.

During this period the cult of Osiris, which had come originally from Syria and had long been practised at Busiris in the Delta, became popular throughout the country, especially in the district around Abydos, where his worship was substituted for that of the jackal-headed Anubis. With this cult came the belief in future rewards and punishments for good and bad deeds performed in this life, thus bringing ethical considerations for the first time into connexion with religious practices.

Hitherto the priests had for the most part been nobles who had carried out priestly duties, except at Heliopolis, where there were priestly families who claimed noble and sometimes royal status. During the Middle Kingdom a class of professional priests arose at the cemeteries to carry out the duties connected with burials and the offerings made to the dead. The temples, also, were served by professional chief priests, though no regular colleges of these had as yet grown up.

BOOKS

BREASTED, J. H. *A History of Egypt* (New York, 1912).
Cambridge Ancient History, vol. i (Cambridge, 1923).
HALL, H. R. *The Ancient History of the Near East* (London, 1920).
MORET, A., and DAVY, G. *From Tribe to Empire* (London, 1926).
MORET, A. *The Nile and Egyptian Civilization* (London, 1927).

13

Chronological Summary

WE must now make a very brief summary of the events recorded in the previous chapters. About the year 2400 B.C., as we pointed out in our last volume, the walls of the Second City of Hissarlik were rebuilt, and that city entered its second phase. About the same time some traders from the Cyclades, who had landed previously in the Gulf of Argolis, settled at the head of the Gulf of Corinth, in a number of villages, founded somewhat earlier by people from Thessaly. The new-comers carried on commerce with the west, with the island of Levkas and the coasts of Italy, and reached the south-east of Sicily, where they introduced the red painted ware that is characteristic of the First Siculan period. Here they seem to have been joined by traders from the south of Crete, who cut in the soft rock tombs, shaped like the interior of a beehive, with small antechambers, in imitation of the *tholoi* that they had erected for generations past on the Mesara Plain.

They extended their voyages still farther to the west and settled at El Argar on the south-east coast of Spain, and soon afterwards in the south of Portugal. Here they worked the rich copper ores in the hills and erected corbelled tombs, with long entrance passages, covered with large mounds of earth.

Then the uncivilized aborigines of the Iberian peninsula, who had up to now been living in an epipalaeolithic condition, learned from the new-comers the arts of agriculture and pot-making. These people made their pots in imitation of the leather bags that they had used for carrying their goods, and thus arose the *Civilisation des Grottes* with its rough pottery. The aborigines did not learn the art of working metal, and copper implements would have been of little use to them, but they made polished axe-heads of crystalline stones, and carried the knowledge of pottery and grain to their neighbours in the south of France, whence this knowledge spread into north Italy. Meanwhile, in places somewhat removed from the coast, the difficulty of erecting corbelled tombs caused the people to build tombs of large upright slabs of stone with one or more capstones on the top. Thus arose, we believe, the custom of erecting circular and polygonal dolmens with or without entrance passages. Before the close of the century the knowledge of grain and pottery seems to have been carried up the Rhône valley into that of the Saône, while the knowledge of metal and the custom of erecting corbelled tombs and dolmens was taken by sea to Le Morbihan in the south of Brittany.

The impression derived from a study of the finds is that this spread of trading activities was a rapid one, and we would provisionally allow twenty-five years for each stage, i.e. from the Gulf of Corinth to Sicily and from there to the islands and the coasts still farther west, and a further period of about the same length before their influence became felt in the interior of the peninsula. We are thus inclined to date the last-named phase about 2300 B.C.

Allowing a century for the spread of this culture northwards from Spain, it would have been about 2200 B.C. that the rough pottery of the Saône valley was carried into Switzerland, where it is known as the *westische Keramik*; then the knowledge of pottery seems to have been taken into northern France, where it spread over a wide area from Belgium to the Bay of Biscay. The century had not far advanced before this civilization had been carried across the Channel to England, and we cannot believe that more than another generation elapsed before the settlement at Windmill Hill near Avebury was founded; it did not last very long, for it was abandoned for a time towards the close, let us suppose, of the same century.

It was about 2200 B.C., too, that the custom of making beaker pottery arose, we believe, somewhere in eastern Galicia or in the Ukraine, though some writers place its origin in Spain. It seems likely, moreover, that its makers formed some kind of trading community, which was associated, we believe, with the activities of Hissarlik II. We cannot but think that there is some link here; Hissarlik II was interested in central Europe, and the beaker culture arose during the third and last chief phase of the life of that great city, while it vanished soon after its disappearance. At the same time the beaker-folk, in our opinion, were clearly not Hissarlik people, but merely some association, widespread on the opener lands of central and western Europe, quite possibly herdsmen and traders.

These beaker-folk seem to have travelled in many directions in their endeavour to get into touch with the sea-traders, whose activities we have already described, for, after what is not likely to have been more than half a century, that is about 2150 B.C., we find evidence of their presence, not only in Moravia and Bohemia, but in Spain and Portugal, and a little later in Denmark, where the custom of erecting dolmens had by this time arrived by way of Ireland and the sea around the north of Scotland. In Denmark the beakers are found associated with an intrusive culture, known as the civilization of the single-graves, that had arrived in Jutland from the south-east. By about 2100 B.C. beakers had passed from Portugal to Brittany and from Bohemia down the Rhine valley to Holland, in the north of which country the practice of building megaliths had already arrived from Denmark. In the meantime the *westische Keramik* had developed in Switzerland into Michelsberg civilization, with its tulip-shaped vases, which spread eastwards into Württemberg and beyond, and northwards as far as Belgium.

In 2169 B.C. Sumu-abu, chief of the invading Amurru, made himself master of Babylon and founded the First Dynasty of that city, while about 2160 B.C. Intef I founded the Eleventh Dynasty of Egypt and brought the period of disorder in that country to an end. At the same time a period of increased prosperity arose in Crete, ushering in the First Middle Minoan period, when the old centres in the east end of the island declined in importance and those in the south came under the leadership of Phaestos; while in the north there arose the palace-city of Knossos, which became a maritime capital of the southern Aegean, but does not seem to have been interested in the western trade, as were, apparently, the earlier southern centres.

It must have been a little before 2100 B.C. that the people of Hissarlik, who had been obtaining copper from the Erzgebirge, where tin also is found, discovered that by adding about 10 per cent. of the latter metal to the former an alloy was produced that was much harder than either of the metals and was, moreover, capable of being cast in closed moulds. Though doubtless this new process was kept a trade secret by the men of Hissarlik, bronze axe-heads and daggers were carried to Crete, and thence to Sicily and Spain, and had probably reached Brittany some time before the close of the century. At the same time the people of Silesia, not far from the Erzgebirge, began to make implements of copper and, a little later, to add a little tin to harden the metal.

Meanwhile, with the development of the Michelsberg civilization the lake-dwellers of Switzerland had passed from the Lower to the Middle Neolithic phase, while the beaker-folk, carrying their characteristic pots, had passed from Holland to England, and early in the twenty-first century had reached Wiltshire. Here we find evidence of their presence in the second period of occupation at Windmill Hill, after the site had lain unoccupied for some years, or, at an estimate, about 2075 B.C., allowing that it had been neglected for about a generation. About the same time the West Kennet ware and the custom of erecting long barrows must have reached England.

In 2067 B.C. Hammurabi succeeded to the kingdom of Babylon, and gradually brought under his sway all the land of Mesopotamia, including Assyria, bringing to an end the kingdoms of Larsa and Isin. Before the close of the century, however, Samsu-iluna, his son, had lost most of this territory, and there arose near the Persian Gulf a new power, known as the Kingdom of the Sea Country. It was probably at the fall of the kingdom of Larsa in 2036 B.C. that Abram left Ur of the Chaldees and migrated to Haran.

About 2000 B.C. the Eleventh Dynasty in Egypt gave way to the Twelfth, and for more than two centuries the land of the Nile enjoyed its second great period of prosperity. The First Dynasty of Babylon lingered on, a shadow of what it had been in the time of Hammurabi, while the almost illiterate kings of the Sea Country ruled most of the Sumerian cities. Hissarlik and Crete grew rich with the profits from their trade in bronze, which was now reaching most parts of Europe readily accessible from the sea. It was probably during this twentieth century that the first flat axes of this alloy reached England.

Shortly before 1900 B.C. there seems to have been another

irruption from the south Russian steppe, for there is slight evidence of fresh intruders into Hungary from that region at this time. It may be that it was a party of these nomads that destroyed the Second City of Hissarlik, for it was sacked and burned at this date. Some think that the destroyers came from the east, for shortly before 1900 B.C. we find a king, Labarnas, welding together the peoples in the centre of Asia Minor to form what afterwards became the Hittite Empire.

After the destruction of the city the mound of Hissarlik was deserted for many centuries, save that a succession of humble villages arose on the site. Trade from Hissarlik was thus at an end, and soon afterwards the activities of the beaker-folk came to a close also, though they continued to make their characteristic pottery in Britain for some centuries. The fall of Hissarlik did not, however, affect the trade of Crete, which became if anything more prosperous, and now entered its Second Middle Minoan period. Meanwhile, life and organization in central and western Europe seems to have developed considerably in a semi-independent fashion. We note the special local developments of megalithic culture in the different regions affected, and we think that the bronze-founder's art established itself in various centres, probably earlier in central than in western Europe. This ushered in the true Bronze Age with its numerous local cultures and its various types of axes, pots, and other objects.

Egypt under its Twelfth Dynasty continued to prosper, but the state of Mesopotamia was going from bad to worse. In 1870 B.C. the Hittites descended the Euphrates and captured Babylon, bringing its First Dynasty to an end, and the whole country remained in a state of disorganization for nearly two centuries.

In 1788 B.C. Queen Sebeknefrure, the last monarch of the Twelfth Dynasty in Egypt, married Khutouire Ugafa, who in her right ascended the throne as first monarch of the Thirteenth Dynasty. His succession to the throne was disputed, and the kingdom was riven asunder. The dynasty ruled a much divided land, with diminishing prosperity, until 1660 B.C., when a horde of Asiatics, who arrived in the Delta at the close of the Twelfth Dynasty, conquered the whole land, where they set themselves up as monarchs of the Sixteenth Dynasty. These were known as the Hyksos or Shepherd Kings.

INDEX